Adonis

A TIME BETWEEN
ASHES & ROSES

POEMS

*Translation, Critical Arabic Edition,
& Afterword by Shawkat M. Toorawa*

With a Foreword by Nasser Rabbat

Syracuse University Press

Mohamad El-Hindi Books on Arab Culture and Islamic Civilization
are published with the assistance of a grant from Ahmad El-Hindi.

Publication of this edition has also been made possible through gener-
ous subventions from the Hull Memorial Publication Fund, Cornell
University; the John S. Knight Institute for Writing in the Disciplines,
Cornell University; and the Department of Near Eastern Studies,
Cornell University.

The paper used in this publication meets the minimum requirements of
American National Standard for Information Sciences—Permanence of
Paper for Printed Library Materials, ANSI Z39.48–1984.∞™

Library of Congress Cataloging-in-Publication Data

[Adūnīs, 1930–

    [Waqt bayna al-ramād wa-al-ward. English]

    A time between ashes and roses : poems / Adonis ; translation, crit-
ical Arabic edition, and afterword by Shawkat M. Toorawa with a fore-
word by Nasser Rabbat.— 1st ed.

    p. cm. — (Middle East literature in translation)

    Includes bibliographical references.

    ISBN 0-8156-0828-4 (alk. paper)

    I. Toorawa, Shawkat M. II. Title. III. Series.

    PJ7862.AA519W313 2004

    892.7´16—dc22

    2004021127

A TIME BETWEEN ASHES & ROSES

Middle East Literature in Translation
Michael Beard and Adnan Haydar, Series Editors

Other titles in Middle East Literature in Translation

〜

The Author and His Doubles: Essays on Classical Arabic Culture.
Abdelfattah Kilito; Michael Cooperson, trans.

The Committee. Sonallah Ibrahim; Mary St. Germain
and Charlene Constable, trans.

A Cup of Sin: Selected Poems. Simin Behbahani;
Farzaneh Milani and Kaveh Safa, trans.

In Search of Walid Masoud: A Novel. Jabra Ibrahim Jabra;
Roger Allen and Adnan Haydar, trans.

Sleeping in the Forest: Stories and Poems. Sait Faik;
Edited by Talat S. Halman

Three Tales of Love and Death. Out el Kouloub

Women without Men: A Novella. Shahrnush Parsipur;
Kamran Talattof and Jocelyn Sharlet, trans.

Yasar Kemal on His Life and Art. Eugene Lyons Hébert
and Barry Tharaud, trans.

Zanouba: A Novel. Out el Kouloub; Nayra Atiya, trans.

For
Parvine,
Maryam, and Asiya

و اصدّر كتابي هذا مستعينا بالله وراغبا اليه

There is Arabic poetry before Adonis,

and there is Arabic poetry after Adonis.

—*Samuel Hazo*

ADONIS, author of more than fifty books of poetry, translation, and criticism, is one of the world's great writers, intellectuals, and cultural critics. In his seventies, he continues to write and to be honored internationally for his work.

SHAWKAT M. TOORAWA is assistant professor of Arabic literature and Islamic Studies in the Department of Near Eastern Studies at Cornell University. He is coauthor of *Interpreting the Self: Autobiography in the Arabic Literary Tradition* and author of *Ibn Abi Tahir Tayfur and Arabic Writerly Culture*.

CONTENTS

FOREWORD

Nasser Rabbat

In the old days of the Arabs, a poet spoke for his tribe. He celebrated its glories, honored its heroes, and denounced its enemies. That was his social function. A poet, however, was also a venerated magician of language. In the pursuit of poetry, he manipulated the expressive potential of words and explored the structural capacity of rhythm. His poems were the vocal signs of his genius (a word ultimately derived from the Arabic *jinni,* the spiritual being often thought to inspire the poet). In fact, despite its prevalent political significance, poesy for the Arabs stood somewhere between human creativity and supernatural revelation.

Today, poetry is still the most captivating form of expression for the Arabs, and poets are still their most eloquent spokespersons. But poets invoke more than the tribe and its exploits. They sing for the nation, the land, the language, the people, the history, and the best among them sing for humanity. It is with the latter that Adonis belongs. A singular, intense, and profoundly cerebral sculptor of words and images, Adonis represents the epitome of Arab humanism. I stress Arab here not because of his birthplace, Syria, the cradle of Arabism, but because he intimately identifies with the Arabic language as his absolute and only homeland; and I use humanist because Adonis mines history for some of its most paradox-ical universalistic and chauvinistic moments and uses them to punctuate a revolutionary poetry committed to the values of pluralism, freedom, enlightenment, and the inevitability of change. In other words, Adonis carves his distinct poetic modernity out of a critical engagement with the past, an engagement that he qualifies as "emanation from the past."

This acute historical consciousness has accompanied Adonis in his long literary journey, which spans fifty years and numerous books of verse and prose. In inchoate form, it animated both his early poetry and political commitment in the 1950s. It then formed the contours of his theoretical and critical search, which culminated in his 1973 Ph.D. dissertation on the Arabic literary tradition, revised and published in four volumes as *al-Thabit wal-Mutahawwil* (The static and the changing). Mature and repeatedly tested in poem after poem, it lately reappeared in *al-Kitab* (The book), which Adonis attributes to his guide and alter ego, the great al-Mutanabbi, while shrewdly assuming the role of the commentator on the fictitious text of the old master. The foundational tenets of poetic tradition have thus achieved an exquisite Adonisian transformation. They no longer only substantiate the modernity of Adonis's poetry. They also anchor its historicity and proclaim its illustrious genealogy.

This does not mean that Adonis's poetic trajectory has been linear or predictable. On the contrary: like all great modern poets, Adonis has been painfully aware of and ingenious in conscripting his own contradictions, shifting views, and impossible dreams in the articulation of his poetry. He, ever the individual speaker for the collective, has suffered each and every setback and radical displacement in contemporary Arab history, and reproduced his anguish in verse as reflections on history, culture, and the tragic human condition. The most disastrous of these debacles was the 1967 Arab-Israeli war and the loss of the rest of Palestine to Israel. Not only was the defeat complete and humiliating to the Arabs, it also exposed the fragility of the political and social programs of the 1960s (chief among them the Nasserite project of socialism and pan-Arabism). The 1967 *naksa* (relapse), as it came to be known, dashed the hopes of an entire generation of educated and motivated Arab nationalists of achieving liberation, unification, and progress.

The 1967 *naksa* also marked a turning point in Adonis's poetry. After what seems to be a period of deep rumination, he published *Waqt bayn al-Ramad wal-Ward* (A time between ashes and roses) in 1970, clearly as his own response to the *naksa*. Initially comprising two long poems, "Muqaddima li-Tarikh Muluk al-Tawaʾif" (Introduction to the history of the petty kings), and "Hadha Huwa Ismi" (This is my name), the collection has been read on different levels. First and foremost, however, it is one of Adonis's most sweeping indictments of contemporary Arabic society, politics, and culture, not only for a tacit responsibility for the *naksa,* but also for an inability to break away from constrictive notions of tradition. In both poems, he grapples with alternating feelings of hope and despair to envision a new future, a future freed from all the moribund ties to the past, all the while retaining a meaningful bond to language. In one especially resounding stanza, he wonders, "How can I make myself clear and in what language? This language that suckles me betrays me/ I will purify it and live on the edge of a time that has died, I walk along the edge of a time that has not come . . ."

The addition of "Qabr min Ajl New York" (A grave for New York), one of Adonis's most discussed poems, to a second edition of *A Time Between Ashes and Roses* issued in 1972 altered the feel of the whole collection. The new poem is a melancholy dialogue with New York upon Adonis's first encounter with it, and ultimately a love letter to Beirut, his adoptive city. It brought with it a new set of themes engendered by the image of the City that Adonis gleaned from his readings, especially of

Walt Whitman, and his lived experience. But the poem also widened the scope of the central question that continues to occupy Adonis until today: how to negotiate the place of history, ethics, and culture in a fast-moving and inevitable modernity. New York offered him the opportunity to treat the question away from the familiar bounds of his own history and culture. He responded brilliantly.

Appending "A Grave for New York" to the collection seems to be a recognition on Adonis's part of crossing from the cultural to the universal dimension of poetry. Indeed, as he himself prophesied when he wrote the first two poems, he was standing in between—between the self and the group, the past and the future, history and modernity, and patriotism and humanism. He knew he was in transition, anticipating his own transformation, which he understood but still did not elucidate. The third poem suggests a path which Adonis will henceforth follow in his continuous striving to articulate his own poetic language. He will enlist the world as his domain of expression, and he will begin with no less than the world's most powerful cultural and political capital.

Making this collection available to the English reader in its entirety is thus a most welcome decision, for it signals the emergence of Adonis as a world poet. But this is not only a historically or biographically important text, it is above all a collection of poems that need to be relished for their lyricism and symbolism. Translating Adonis's enigmatic verses is already a difficult task. Capturing his imagery and his poetry's innate rhythm is a true achievement. Shawkat Toorawa succeeds in both. He does so by sensibly assimilating the literary style of Adonis, what is deferentially called in Arabic, *al-sahl al-mumtani*ᶜ, meaning the apparently easy but effectively sublime. Like the original Arabic verses, Toorawa's elegant and faithful translation effortlessly and tastefully infuses both the mind and ear of the reader, even when it is only read silently. It is poetry in its own right.

TRANSLATOR'S PREFACE

Adonis is arguably the greatest living Arab poet and also one of the world's most influential literary critics and cultural theorists. He has been producing poetry, criticism, translations, and anthologies for fifty years. This is why I chose to translate Adonis.

As for my choice of collection, the basis for the selection is three-fold. First, *A Time Between Ashes and Roses* had a major impact on the course of Arabic poetry when it first appeared in 1970 and especially when it was reissued in revised form in 1972. Second, in spite of its vintage, *A Time Between Ashes and Roses* remains for Adonis a signature work, embodying a great deal of what he has been striving for in his criticism, poetry, editorial and anthological activity, and personal and public example. At a poetry recitation at the Cairo Book Fair in 1989, Adonis's sole reading was of "Introduction to the History of the Petty Kings," the first of the three long poems in the collection. Third, because he is seen as a poet difficult to understand, Adonis's writing in general, and his long poems in particular, including those in *A Time Between Ashes and Roses,* have not been well served by English-language scholarship and translation.

Until 1990, two decades after *A Time Between Ashes and Roses* first appeared, only a poem later added by Adonis to the collection, "A Grave for New York," had piqued the interest of Anglophone translators, although short extracts and segments of the other two poems did exist in a few anthologies and critical works. It is a pleasure, therefore, to be able to provide a translation of the entire 1972 collection, comprising "Introduction to the History of the Petty Kings," "This Is My Name," and "A Grave for New York." As the 1972 edition and rescension of *A Time Between Ashes and Roses* (*Waqt bayna al-ramad wa al-ward* [Beirut: Dar al-ʿAwda, 1972]) is the one which most widely circulated, that is the one I have provided, with identical spacing and formatting, on the facing Arabic pages. The translations themselves also replicate as closely as possible the spacing, punctuation, and page breaks of Adonis's text, partly in an attempt to do away with what the poet Charles Péguy regarded as the destruction and alteration of a translated text.

I have placed all the critical material in this volume *after* the poems, keeping notes to an absolute minimum. The Afterword and Selected Bibliography are for those wishing to learn more about Adonis, his poetry, and this collection. For unfamiliar names and words, the Glossary in the back following the two appendixes should be consulted. These critical aids are positioned behind the primary text to allow the reader, who so wishes, to experience the poetry unburdened by my interventions—other than the (inevitable) act of translation.

Adonis has described the 1996 edition of his complete poetical works (*al-Aʿmal al-shiʿriyya al-kamila,* 3 vols. [Damascus: Dar al-Mada li al-Thaqafah wa al-Nashr, 1996]) as definitive. For specialists interested in the differences between the 1972 and 1996 rescensions, I have placed in square brackets [ ] the Arabic material that is omitted in the 1996 edition; indicated any additions (very few indeed) with a caret ^; and placed material that has been emended between angle brackets < >. These changes are also detailed in Appendix A. And, as the poems of *A Time Between Ashes and Roses* have appeared in several editions, I provide a publication history in Appendix B.

ACKNOWLEDGMENTS

I began work on these translations while a graduate student at the University of Pennsylvania and have tinkered with them over the years: while in Cairo as a fellow at the American Research Center in Egypt, while teaching at Duke University and the University of Mauritius, and while a Fellow at Harvard University's W. E. B. DuBois Institute. The volume took final shape at Cornell University.

I thank the following parties: the American Association of Teachers of Arabic for recognizing the value of earlier incarnations of the translations and the *Journal of Arabic Literature* for publishing them (and for graciously allowing me to revise them substantially and publish them here); David Hirsch, Iman Mersal, and Carmen Sue Cross of *adabiyat-l* and Elie Chelala of *aljadid* for references; Shelly Marino for tireless technical help; Annette Hagan of Edinburgh University Library, Michael Hopper of Widener Library at Harvard University, and especially Ali Houissa of Olin Library at Cornell University, all of whom obtained materials for me with alacrity, expertise, and good cheer.

I must also single out for special thanks: Adonis, who gave me permission to translate and publish this collection and who has kept patient faith in my engagement with it; Roger Allen, for having introduced me and attuned me to the splendors of Arabic poetry; Adnan Haydar and Michael Beard for embracing and nurturing this project since its inception, for carefully reviewing the translations, and for making innumerable discerning and intuitive suggestions; and Ross Brann, for the support that has made the completion of this project, and so many other things, possible. Nasser Rabbat, like Adonis a major Arab intellectual, graciously agreed to write the foreword; Iftikhar and Elizabeth Dadi, gifted artists like Adonis, produced the beautiful cover. In addition, the translations have benefited from the intuition and insight of Kristen Brustad, miriam cooke, John Ledoux, Joseph Lowry, Marc Ostfield, the anonymous reviewers of Syracuse University Press, Dwight Reynolds, RRAALL, Devin Stewart, Abbas al-Tonsi, and Herb Wolfson.

I am grateful to everyone at Syracuse University Press, in particular Anne Carlson, Theresa Litz, Mary Peterson Moore, Michael Rankin, and the ever-delightful Mary Selden Evans, whose indefatigable support, unflagging commitment to this project, and infectious warmth eased the publication process.

For subvention toward the cost of publication, I am deeply grateful to benefactors at Cornell University: the John S. Knight Program for Writing in the Disciplines, and its director, Jonathan Monroe; the Hull Memorial Publication Fund, and its chair, J. Ellen Gainor; and the Department of Near Eastern Studies, and its chair, Ross Brann. By financially supporting this volume, these institutions and individuals not only demonstrate their commitment to world literature but also confer distinction on the volume.

I thank my parents for so much, including teaching me to love poetry and to pursue my passions. And I thank my wife, Parvine Bahemia, for her sustaining companionship and love. I dedicate this work to her, and to our children, Maryam and Asiya, translations of us as it were.

A TIME BETWEEN

ASHES & ROSES

POEMS

مقدمة لتاريخ ملوك الطوائف

[تحية لجمال عبد الناصر ، أول قائد عربي
حديث عمل لكي ينتهي عصر ملوك
الطوائف ويبتدىء العصر الآخر .]

AN INTRODUCTION

TO THE HISTORY OF

THE PETTY KINGS

*A greeting to Gamal Abdel Nasser, the first
modern Arab leader who worked to bring
an end to the age of the Petty Kings and to
begin another age.*

وجهُ يافا طفلٌ / هل الشجرُ الذابل يزهو ؟ هل تدخل
الأرضُ في صورة عذراء؟/ مَن هناك يرجّ الشرقَ ؟/جاء العصف
الجميلُ و لم يأتِ الخرابُ الجميلُ / صوتٌ شريدٌ... /

(كان رأسٌ يهذي يهرّجُ محمولاً ينادي أنا الخليفةُ) /
هاموا حفروا حفرةً لوجه عليّ / كان طفلاً و كان أبيض
أو أسودَ ، يافا أشجارهُ و أغانيه و يافا ... / تكدّسو ،
مزّقوا وجه عليّ /
دمُ الذبيحة في الأقداحِ ، قولوا : جبّانةٌ ،
لا تقولوا : كان شعري وردًا و صار دماءً ،

nakban = my disastr

The face of Jaffa is a child / How can withered trees blossom? Has
the Earth taken on the image of a virgin? / Who is there to shake the
East? / The beautiful storm has come but not the beautiful devastation
/ A fugitive voice . . . /

(A head, borne aloft, babbled, talked deliriously, calling out "I am the
Caliph")* / They wandered, and prepared an ambush for the face of
Ali / He was a child, a white child, or a black child, Jaffa was his
trees and his songs, Jaffa . . . / They pressed together, they rent apart
the face of Ali /

> The blood of the sacrificial victim is in the drinking cups. Say:†
> Mass graves, Do not say: My poetry was a rose and became blood

*A phrase occurred here in the first edition (1970) which has been dropped
from all subsequent editions: "in Fustat in the presence of the troops." Fustat was
the first city to be founded in Egypt by the Muslims in the seventh century, the fu-
ture Old Cairo.

†The addressee is plural here. Adonis switches person frequently, something
difficult to convey unobtrusively in English but which I have attempted wherever
possible. Another common switch is between the perfect and imperfect tenses.

ليس بين الدماء
والورد إلا خيط شمسٍ ، قولوا : رمادي بيتُ
وابنُ عبّادَ يشحذ السيفَ بين الرأس والرأس وابنُ جَهْوَرَ
ميْتُ .

لم يكن في البدايه
غير جذْرٍ من الدمع / أعني بلادي
والمدى خيطيَ – انْقطعتُ وفي الخضرة العربيه
غرقت شمسيَ / الحضارةُ نَقَالةٌ والمدينه
وردةٌ وثنيَّه –
خيمةُ :
هكذا تبدأ الحكايةُ أو تنتهي الحكايَه .

There is nothing between blood
And rose but a thread of sun. Say: My ashes are a dwelling place
Ibn Abbad sharpens his sword between one head and another, and
Ibn Jahwar is Dead.

In the beginning there was nothing
But the root of tears / I mean my country
And the expanse was my thread—I was torn free and in the Arab
greenness my sun was drowned / Civilization is a vehicle for the
wounded and the city is a pagan rose,
A tent:

So the story begins, or so the story ends

والمدى خيطيَ – اتّصلتُ أنا الفوهةَ الكوكبيه ْ
وكتبتُ المدينه
(حينما كانت المدينة مقطورةً والنواحْ
سورُها البابليُّ) ، كتبت المدينه ْ
مثلما تنضحُ الأبجديّه ْ
لا لكي ألأَمَ الجراحْ
لا لكي أبعث المومياءْ
بل لكي أبعث الفروقَ . . . / الدماءْ
تجمعُ الوردَ والغرابَ / لكي أقطع الجسور
ولكي أغسل الوجوه الحزينه
بنزيف العصورْ . .

[9]

The expanse was my thread—I, the astral crater, I reconnected
And I wrote the city
(while the city was being dragged along and lamentation was its
    Babylonian walls), I wrote the city
Just as the alphabet flows
Not to heal a wound
Not to reawaken the mummy
But to arouse differences . . . / Blood
Unites roses and ravens / To cleave the bridges
To bathe the grieving faces
In the hemorrhage of ages

و كتبت المدينه
مثلما يذهب النبيّ إلى الموت / أعني بلادي
و بلادي الصّدى
والصّدى والصّدى ...

كشفتْ رأسها البَاءُ ، والجيمُ خصلةُ شَعْرٍ ، إنْقرضْ إنْقرضْ
ألفٌ أولُ الحروف إنْقرضْ إنْقرضْ
أسمعُ الهاءَ تنشج والراءُ مثل الهلالْ
غارقاً ذائباً في الرمالْ
إنْقرضْ إنْقرضْ

And I wrote the city
as a prophet goes to death / I mean my country
    My country is the echo
    The echo, the echo . . .

The letter *bâ* uncovered her head, *jîm* is a lock of hair: Perish, perish . . .
Alif is the first letter: Perish, perish . . .
I hear the letter *hâ* sobbing; and *râ* is like the crescent moon
Immersed, dissolving in the sands.
Perish, perish

*destruction /
creation* [handwritten annotation]

يا دماً يتخثّر يجري صحارَى كلامْ
يا دماً ينسج الفجيعة أو ينسج الظلامْ
إنْقرض إنْقرض

سحرُ تاريخكَ انتهى
ادفنوا وجهَه الذليلَ وموروثَهُ الأبْلَها
واعْذري واغْفري
يا قرونَ الغزالاتِ ، يا أعينَ المها . . .

O blood, coagulating, flowing like deserts of speech
O blood, weaving calamity or weaving darkness
Perish, perish . . .

The magic of your history has ended
Bury its servile face and doltish inheritance
Forgive and pardon
You gazelle-horns . . . you wild antelope eyes . . .

أحارُ ، كلَّ لحظةٍ أراكِ يا بلادي
في صورةٍ ،
أحملكِ الآنَ على جبيني ، بين دمي وموتي : أأنتِ مقبره
أم وردةٌ ؟

أراكِ أطفالاً يجرجرون
أحشاءَهم ، يُصغونَ يسجدون°
للقيد ، يلبسون°
لكل سوطٍ جلده° . . . أمقبره°
أم وردةٌ ؟

قَتلتِني قتلتِ أغنياتي
أأنتِ مجزرَه°
أم ثورةٌ ؟
أحارُ ، كلَّ لحظةٍ أراكِ يا بلادي في صورةٍ . . .

I am confused, my country, every time I see you
    In a different shape. Now I carry you
on my forehead, between my blood and my death: Are you a graveyard
    Or a rose?
I see you as children, dragging their
entrails along, obedient, prostrating themselves
    To their own shackles, wearing
    A different skin for each whiplash . . . A graveyard
    Or a rose?

You killed me, you killed my songs
    Are you just carnage
    Or a revolution?

I am confused, my country, every time I see you in a different shape . . .

وعليّ يسأل الضوءَ ، ويضيء
حاملاً تاريخه المقتولَ من كوخٍ لكوخٍ :
علّموني أنّ لي بيتاً كبيتي في أريحا
أنّ لي في القاهره
إخوةٌ ، أنّ حدود الناصره
مكةً .
كيف استحالَ العلمُ قيداً ؟
ألهذا يرفض التاريخ وجهي ؟
ألهذا لا أرى في الأفق شمساً عربيه؟ ؟

Ali questions the light and leaves
Carrying his murdered history from hut to hut:
 "They taught me that I have a house like my house in Jericho
 That I have in Cairo
 Brothers, that the boundaries of Nazareth are
 Mecca.
 How did knowledge transform into shackles?
 Is this why history refuses my face
 Why I no longer see an Arab sun on the horizon?"

آهِ لو تعرف المهزله
(سمِّها خطبةَ الخليفة ِ أو سمِّها المهرجان°)
ولها قائدان°
واحدٌ يَشحذُ المقصله°
واحدٌ يتمرّغُ . . . لو تعرف المهزله°

كيف ، أينَ انْسللت°
‹في حصار المذابح . . . ماذا› ، قُتِلت° ؟

Oh, if you only knew the comedy
(Call it the Caliph's sermon, or call it a festival)
It has two directors:
One sharpens the guillotine
The other wallows in dust . . . If only you knew the comedy

How, where, did you sneak in?
Past the walls surrounding the slaughter . . . What, were you butchered?

[أنظرِ الآنَ كيف انتهيتَ ولم تنتهِ المهزلهْ
مُتُّ كالآخرينْ
مثلما ينشجُ الدهرُ في رنة السالفينْ
مثلما يكسر الغيم أبوابه القُزَحيّهْ
مثلما يغرق الماءُ في الرمل ِ أو تقطعُ الأبديهْ
عُنُقَ القُبّرهْ]

كنتَ كالآخرين ، انْتهيتَ و لم تنتهِ المهزلهْ
كنتَ كالآخرينَ – ارفض ِ الآخرينْ

[15]

See now: you ended but the comedy did not
You have died like all the others
Like time sobbing in the lungs of our forefathers
Like clouds breaking their rainbow doors
Like water sinking into sand, like eternity breaking
        the neck of the lark

You were like the others; you ended and the comedy did not
You were like the others—Deny the others

بدأوا من هناكَ ابتدىءَ من هُنا
حول طفلٍ يموت°
حول بيتٍ تهدَّم فاستعمرته البيوت°

وابتدىء من هنا
من أنين الشوارع من ريحها الخانقه
من بلادٍ يصير اسمها مقبره
وابتدىء من هنا
مثلما تبدأ الفجيعةُ أو تُولد الصاعقه°

They began from there. You, begin from here
Around a child who is dying
Around a demolished house, occupied and taken over by other houses

Begin from here
From the moans of the streets
From their suffocating odor
From a country whose name has become a graveyard
Begin from here, just as calamity begins or as the thunderbolt is born

مُتَّ ؟ هاصرتَ كالرعد في رَحِم الصّاعقه
بارئاً مثلما تَبرأُ الصاعقه
أنظرْ الآنَ كيف انصهرتَ و كيف انبعثتَ ، انتهيتَ ولم
تنته الصاعقهْ .

أعرفُ ، كان ملككَ الوحيدَ ظلَّ خيمةٍ ، و كان فيها خرقٌ ،
و مرّةً يكونُ ماءٌ مرةً رغيفٌ ، وكان أطفالك يكبرونْ
في بُركةٍ ،

[17]

Did you die? See, how you've become like thunder in a womb
of thunderbolts absolving like thunder absolves
See how you have melted away and how you have been resurrected.
You have ended but the thundering has not

I know your only possession was the shadow of a tent. In it were
rags, sometimes water, sometimes a loaf of bread, and your children
    grew up in a puddle

لم تَيْأس انتفضْتَ صرتَ الحلمَ والعيونْ
تظهرُ في كوخٍ على الأردنّ أو في غَزّةٍ والقدْسْ
تقتحمُ الشارعَ وهو مَأتَمٌ تتركه كالعرْسْ

وصوتُك الغامرُ مثلُ بحرٍ
ودمُكَ النافرُ مثلُ جَبلٍ

وحينما تحملك الأرضُ إلى سريرها
تترك للعاشقِ للآحقِ جدولينْ
من دمكَ المسفوحِ مرّتينْ .

You did not give up hope, you rebelled, you became the dream, the eyes
Appearing in a hut along the River Jordan, or in Gaza, in Jerusalem:
Storming the street when it is a funeral ceremony, then leaving it as
a wedding feast

Your all-encompassing voice is like a sea
And your spurting blood like a mountain

And when the Earth carries you to her bed
You leave for the lover and for the successor two streams
Of your twice spilled blood

وجهُ يافا طفلٌ / هل الشجَرُ الذابلُ يزهو ؟ هل تدخل الأرضُ
في صورة عذراءَ ؟ / مَن هناكَ يرجُّ الشرق / جاء العَصْفُ
الجميلُ ولم يأت الخرابُ الجميلُ / صوتٌ شريد ً . . .

سقطَ الماضي ولم يسقطْ (لماذا يسقط الماضي ولا يسقطُ ؟)
دالٌ قامةٌ يكسرها الحزنُ (لماذا يسقط الماضي ولا يسقطُ ؟)
قافُ قابُ قوسين وأُدْنى

أطلبُ الماءَ ويعطينيَ رملاً
أطلب الشمسَ و يعطينيَ كهفاً

The face of Jaffa is a child / How can withered trees blossom? Has
the Earth taken on the image of a virgin? / Who is there to shake the
East? / The beautiful storm has come but not the beautiful devastation
/ A fugitive voice . . .

The past has fallen and yet has not ended
    (Why does the past end yet not end?)
The letter *dâl*, a frame sorrow fractures
    (Why does the past end yet not end?)
The letter *qâf* very close, imminent

I ask for water and I'm given sand
I ask for the sun and I'm given a cave

سيّدٌ أنتَ ؟ ستبقى
سيّداً . عبدٌ ؟ ستبقى
هكذا يُؤْثَرُ ، يعطينيَ كهفاً وأنا أطلبُ شمساً ، فلماذا سقط
الماضي ولم يسقط ؟ لماذا هذه الأرضُ التي تَنْسِلُ أياماً كئيبَه
هذه الأرضُ الرتيبه ْ

سيّدٌ أنتَ ؟ ستبقى
سيّداً . عبدٌ ؟ ستبقى

غيّر الصورةَ لكن سوف تبقى
غيّر الرايةَ لكن سوف تبقى

A master, you? You will remain
A master. A slave? That's what you'll remain
It goes like this: I'm given a cave though I ask for a sun. And why did
the past end and yet not end? Why this Earth, that begets melancholy
days, this monotonous Earth?

A master, you? You will remain
A master. A slave? That's what you'll remain

Change the picture, and yet that's what you'll remain
Change the banner, and yet that's what you'll remain

. . . في خريطةٍ تمتدّ . . . الخ ،
حيث يدخلُ السيّد المقيمُ في الصفحة ١ راكباً حيواناً بحجم
المشنقة ، يتحوّلُ إلى تمثالٍ ملء الساحات العامة . و (كانت)
الحاكمة تغسل عجيزتها وحولها نساءٌ يدخلن في الرمح و يمضغن
بخورَ القصر والرجال يسجّلون دقات قلوبهنّ على زمنٍ يتكوّم
كالخرقة بين الأصابع حيث

ك   ترتجف تحت نواةٍ رفضيّةٍ بعمق الضوء
ت   تاريخٌ مسقوف بالجثث وبخار الصلاة
ا   عمود مشنقة مبلّل بضوءٍ موحل
ب   سكين تكشط الجلد الآدميّ وتصنعه نعلاً لقدمين
      سماويتين في خريطةٍ تمتدّ . . . الخ .

. . . In a map that extends . . . etc.

In which the lingering master enters on page one riding an animal the size of a gallows, transforms into an enormous statue, filling the public spaces. Justice cleans (or used to clean) her buttocks, while women all around her straddle spears and chew palace incense, while men record the women's heartbeats to a time crumpled like tattered rags between the fingers. In which

kâf	trembles beneath a dissenting nucleus deep as light
tâ	is a history roofed with corpses and the vapor of prayers
alif	a gallows moist with a muddy light
bâ	a knife that scrapes off human skin and fashions it into sandals for two heavenly feet, in a map that extends . . . etc.

شجرٌ يُثمرُ التحوّلَ و الهجرةَ
في الضوء جالسٌ في فلسطين و أغصانه نوافذُ / أصغينا
‹لأفراحه› قرأنا معه نجمةَ الأساطير / جندٌ و قضاةٌ يدحرجون
عظاماً و رؤوساً ، و ‹راقدون› كما يرقد حلمٌ يُهَجَّرون يُجَرّونَ
إلى التيه . . . /

كيف نبدأ ،
[من أينَ ، هل البحر قادرٌ ، هل حَنانُ الشمس ؟]
(– يكفيني رغيفٌ
كوخٌ و في الشمس ما يمنح فَيْئاً ، لا لستُ خوذةَ سيّاف
و لا ترسَ سيّدٍ ، أنا نهرُ الأردنّ أُستفردُ الزهورَ و أغويها /
دمٌ نازفٌ / تبطّنتُ أرضي ودمي ماؤها دمي وسيبقى ذلك
الساهر النحيلُ : غبارٌ يمزجُ العاشقَ المشرّدَ بالريحِ ،
ويبقى نسْغٌ /)

Trees, bearing the fruits of change and migration in the light,
are seated in Palestine, their branches windows / We listened to
their celebrations, read with them the star of their legends / Soldiers
and judges rolled bones and heads, corpses sleep as a dream sleeps:
forced out, dragged to trackless wanderings . . . /

How are we to begin?
From where? Is the sea capable, is the sun's compassion?/

(—A loaf and
a hut are all I need. In the sun I will find something that affords me
some shade. No, I am not an executioner's helmet nor a nobleman's
shield: I am the River Jordan, I pick out the flowers and I beguile
them. / Spent blood. / I am absorbed into my land: My blood is its
water, my blood, and that gaunt night-dweller will remain: dust
mixing the fugitive lover with the wind, and sap remains/)

يتمتم طفلٌ ، وجهُ يافا

طفلٌ / [هل الشجَرُ الذابلُ يزهو ؟ /]

(– متى أتوا ؟ كيف لم نشعرْ ؟ جبال الخليل
يدفعها الليل ويمضي والأرضُ تهزأ / لم نشعرْ/ دمٌ نازفٌ /] هنا
سقط الثائرُ / حيفا تئنُ في حجَرٍ اسودَ و النخلة التي فيّأت
مريمَ تبكي/ [حيفا تسافر في عَينيْ قتيلٍ حيفا بحيرة حزن
جرحت قلبها وسالتْ مع الشمس إلينا /] همسْتُ في قدمي
جوعٌ وفي راحتيٍ تضطرب الأرضُ / كشفنا أسرارَنا (بُقَع
الدمع طريقٌ) أجسُّ خاصرة الضوء يجثّ الصحراءَ والكونَ
مربوطاً بحبلٍ من الملائك / هل تشهدُ آثار كوكبٍ ؟ يسمع
الكوكبُ صوتي رويتُ عنه سأروي . . .

A child stammers, the face of Jaffa is a
child / How can withered trees blossom? /

(—When did they come?
How did we not feel it? The night pushes away the mountains of
Hebron and passes away, and the Earth jeers / We did not feel it /
Spent blood / The revolutionary fell here / Haifa groans in a black
rock and the date palm that gave shade to Mary cries / Haifa journeys
in eyes of a victim, Haifa is a lake of sadness, it wounded its heart
and flowed with the sun toward us / I whispered: In my step is
hunger and in my palms the earth trembles / We divulged our secrets
(the stains of our tears are a pathway). I feel someone's waist, light
uproots the desert and the universe, fastened with a rope of angels /
Do you see the relics of a star? The star hears my voice. I have told
of it, I shall tell again . . .)

في الزمن ‹القاتل› شخصٌ رمى تاريخه ‹للنار غطّى مدى وجوهنا
بحمرة الخجلِ›°

ومات /
لن تعرفَ حريةً ما دامت الدولةُ موجودةٌ /

تذكرُ ؟ [كان السجن بوابةً للشمس كان الأملُ°]
تذكرُ ؟ (والقاعده
وسلطة العمالِ . . . .) ما الفائده
تنحدرُ الثورة بعد اسمِه
في لفظةٍ ، تمتدّ في مائِده /
هل تقرأ المائده ؟ /

In the murderous age a person threw his history into the fire, covered
the expanse of our faces with the red blush of ignominy

And died /
You shall not know freedom as long as the State exists /

Do you remember? The prison was a portal to the sun. And
there was hope, do you remember? (The principles
and the power of the workers . . . ?) What's the use?
The revolution, after you mention his name,
Is reduced to an expression, spread onto a table /
Have you read "The Table Spread"? /

كان فدائيٌّ يخطّ اسمه ناراً و في الخناجر البارده
يموتُ/
والقدسُ تخطّ اسمها :
لم تزل الدولةُ موجودةٌ
لم تزل الدولةُ موجودةٌ .

غيرَ أنَّ النهَرَ المذبوحَ يجري :
كلّ ماءٍ وجه يافا
كلُّ جرحٍ وجه يافا

A freedom fighter traces his name in fire, and in the frozen throats
    He dies /
    Jerusalem traces her name:
    The State still exists
    The State still exists.

Even so, the butchered river flows:
    All water is the face of Jaffa
    Every wound the face of Jaffa

والملايين التي تصرخُ : كلا ، وجه يافا
والأحبّاء على الشُّرفة أو في القيد أو في القبر يافا
والدمُ النازفُ من خاصرة العالم يافا

سمِّني قيساً وسمِّ الأرض ليلى
باسْم يافا
باسْم شعبٍ شرّدته البشريه ْ
سمِّني قنبلةً أو بندقيه ْ . . .

And the millions screaming "Never!" are the face of Jaffa
And the beloved ones on the balcony, in shackles, in the graves, are Jaffa
And the spent blood from the waist of the world is Jaffa

    Call me Qays, call the earth Layla
    In the name of Jaffa
    In the name of a people made destitute by humanity
    Call me a bomb or a rifle . . .

هذا أنا : لا ، لستُ من عصر الأفولْ
أنا ساعةُ الهتْك العظيم أتت وخلخلة العقولْ
هذا أنا – عبرَتْ سحابه
حبلى بزوبعة الجنونْ
والتيهُ يَمرق تحت نافذتي ، يقول الآخرونْ :
ٓ يرعى قطيع جفونه
يصل الغرابةَ بالغرابةْ

هذا أنا أصلُ الغرابةَ بالغرابهْ

This is what I am: No, I am not from the age of the decline
I am the hour of dreadful agitation and shaking loose of minds
This is what I am—A cloud passed by
Pregnant with a hurricane of madness
Ostentation rushes by beneath my window. The others say:
    "He tends the herd of his eyelids,
    He unites strangeness with strangeness."

This is what I am: Uniting strangeness with strangeness

أرّختُ : فوق المئذنه'

قمرٌ يسوس الأحصنه'

وينام بين يدَيْ' تميمه

و ذكرتُ : بقّعت الهزيمه

جَسدَ العصورْ'

وَهرانُ مثل الكاظميّه'

و دمشق بيروت العجوزْ

صحراءُ تزدردُ الفصولَ ، دمٌ تعفّنَ – لم تعد نارُ الرموزْ'

تلد المدائن والفضاء ، ذكرتُ لم تكن البقيّه

إلا دماً هَرِماً يموت يموتُ بقّعت الهزيمه

جسدَ العصورْ' .

I chronicled: Atop the minaret
             Is a moon guiding the stallions,
             Asleep beneath the influence of an amulet.
I recorded: The defeat stained
          The body of the times
Oran is like Kazimiyya
Damascus is old Beirut
Deserts swallowing seasons, blood putrefying—No longer does the
fire of symbols give birth to cities, to space. I recorded: What
remained was nothing but decrepit blood dying, dying. The defeat
    stained the body of the times.

. . . في خريطة تمتدّ الخ ،

حيث تتحول الكلمة إلى نسيج تعبرُ في مسامّه رؤوسٌ، كالقطن
المنفوش ، أيامٌ تحمل أفخاذاً مثقوبةً تدخل في تاريخٍ فارغٍ إلا
من الاظافر ، مثلثات بأشكال النساء تضطجع بين الورقة
والورقة ؛ كل شيء يدخل إلى الأرض من سُمّ الكلمة ، الحشرةُ
اللهُ الشاعر بالوخز والأرق وحرارة الصوت بالرصاص والوضوء
بالقمر و نملة سليمان بحقولٍ تثمر لافتاتٍ كتب عليها « البحث
عن رغيف » أو « البحث عن عجيزة لكن استتروا » أو « هل
الحركة في الخطوة أم في الطريق ؟ »

والطريقُ رملٌ يتقوّس فوقه الهواء و الخطوة
زمنٌ أملس كالحصاة . . .

[29]

. . . In a map that extends, etc.
In which the word is transformed into a web whose mesh is riddled
with holes like carded cotton, days bearing punctured thighs enter a
history emptied of everything but talons, triangles in the form of
women lying between one page and another. Everything comes to the
earth through the eye of a word: vermin, God, the poet, by puncturing
and by insomnia and by feverish voice, by bullets and ritual ablutions,
by the moon and Solomon's ant, by fields of streamers on which are
written "In search of bread" or "In search of buttocks—but in secret" or
"Is movement in the step or the path?"

The path is sand above which arcs the
wind and the step is time smooth as a pebble . . .

[حيث وقفَ على طرف العمل ، وضع الكتاب كالشامة
على جبينه ورسم جوقةً من الملائكة على شفتيه وأذنيه ، أخذ
يغرز أصابعه و اسنانه في قصعة الكلام طالت أذناه و سقط
شعره و تحول ،] و كان الوقت يشرف أن يصبح خارج الوقت
و ما يسمّونه الوطن يجلس على حافة الزمن يكاد أن يسقط ،
« كيف يمكن إمساكه ؟ » سأل رجل مقيد و شبه ملجوم لم
يجنه الجواب لكن جاءه قيدٌ آخر وأخذ حشد كمسحوق الرمل
يفرز مسافة بحجم لام ميم ألف أو بحجم ص ع ي ه ك و يسير
فيها ينسج رايات و بسطاً و شوارع و قباباً ويبني جسراً يعبر
عليه من الآخرة إلى الأولى . . .

In which he stopped on the edge of the action, he
affixed the book like the birthmark on his forehead and drew a chorus
of angels on his lips and his ears. He began to thrust his fingers and
his teeth into a large bowl of speech, his ears lengthened, and his hair
fell out and changed. Time was about to step out of time, and what
they call the homeland sits on the edge of time about to fall. "How
to hold on to it?" asked a man in shackles, almost bridled. He did not
get an answer, only more shackles, and a crowd like powdered sand
began to survey an expanse the size of the sequence *lâm-mîm-alif* or
the size of *sâd-ʿayn-yâ-hâ-kâf,* walking across it, weaving banners,
carpets, streets, domes, and building a bridge to cross from the
afterlife to this world . . .

حيث عبرت

ذبابةٌ و جلست على الكلمة ، لم يتحركْ حرف ، طارت وقد
استطال جناحاها عبر طفل و سأل عن الكلمة طلع في حنجرته
شوكٌ و أخذ الخرَس يدبّ إلى لسانه . . .

في خريطةٍ تمتدّ . . . الخ ، حيث

« العدو يطغى وهم يخسرون ، و يمدّ وهم يجزرون ، و يطول
وهم يقصرون ، إلى أن عادوا إلى علمٍ ناكسٍ و صوتٍ خافت ،
و انشغل كل ملكٍ بسدّ فتوقه ،

. . . و عندما يجدّ الجد و يطلب الأندلس عون الملك الصالح
لاستخلاص إقليم الجزيرة وقد سقط في ايدي الاسبان يكتفي
بالاسف والتعزية ويقول بانّ الحرب سجال وفي سلامتكم الكفاية،

In which a fly
flew by and sat on the word—not a letter moved. It took to flight,
spreading its wings. A child appeared and asked about the word. A
thorn appeared in his throat and muteness began to overtake his
tongue . . .

In a map that extends . . . etc.

In which "The Enemy prevails, they suffer losses; he presses on, they
retreat; he grows, but they dwindle—to a lowered flag, an inaudible
voice. Every king is busy with the patching up of his holes
. . . When things turn serious, al-Andalus seeks the help of the pious
king in saving the Peninsula fallen into the hands of the Spaniards.
He is content with apologies and condolences and says that war has
its ups and downs and that you should be content with a quick recovery.

... ولم يزل العدو يواثبهم ويكافحهم ويغاديهم القتال ويراوحهم
حتى أجهضهم عن أماكنهم و جفّلهم عن مساكنهم و أركبهم
طبقاً عن طبق واستأصلهم بالقتل والاسر كيفما اتفق ... »

في خريطة تمتد . . . الخ ،
رفض التاريخ المعروف التي يطبخ فوق نار السلطان ان يذكر
شاعراً . . . والبقية آتيةٌ ،
في خريطةٍ تمتدّ . . . الخ ،

يأتي وقتٌ بين الرماد والورد
ينطفئ فيه كل شيء
يبدأ فيه كل شيء .

. . . And the Enemy is still attacking and still battling, time and again, until he has evicted them from their strongholds and scared them away from their homes, piled them up, and exterminated them through murder and captivity, come what may . . ."

In a map that extends . . . etc.
Famous history, cooked upon a fire of power, refused to remember a poet . . . and the rest follows,
In a map that extends . . . etc.

A time between ashes and roses is coming
When everything shall be extinguished
When everything shall begin.

...وأغنّي فجيعتي، لم أعد ألمح نفسي إلا على طرف التاريخ في شفْرةٍ / سأبدأُ ، لكن اين ؟ من اين ؟ كيف أوضح نفسي و بأيّ اللغات ؟ هذي التي أرضع منها تخونني/ سأزكّيها وأحيا على شفير زمانٍ مات أمشي على شفير زمانٍ لم يجىءْ

غيرَ أنني لستُ وحدي

[33]

. . . I sing my own misfortune. I see myself only upon the margin of history, on a blade-edge / I shall begin, but where? From where? How can I make myself clear and in what languages? This language that suckles me betrays me / I shall bear witness to this and live on the edge of a time that has died. I walk along the edge of a time that has not come

Except that I am not alone

...ها غزالُ التاريخ يفتحُ أحشائيَ / نهرُ العبيد يهدرُ ^ [لم يبقَ
نبيّ إلا تصعْلكَ لم يبقَ إلهٌ / نجيء نكتشف الخبز/] اكتشفنا
ضوءاً يقود ألى الأرض اكتشفنا شمساً تجيء من القبضة هاتو فؤوسكم
نحمل ﴿اللهَ﴾ كشيخٍ يموت [نفتح للشمس طريقاً غيرَ المآذن للطفل
كتاباً غيرَ الملائك للحالم عيناً غير المدينة والكوفة / هاتوا
فؤوسكم]

لستُ وحدي . . .

. . . Here is the gazelle of history, opening my entrails / The river of slaves rumbles on. No prophet remains who did not become an idle wanderer, no god remains / We come to discover, discovering bread / We discovered a light leading us to Earth, we discovered a sun coming from the fist. Bring your axes. We carry God like a dying shaykh, we open to the sun a path other than minarets, to the child a book other than angels, to the dreamer an eye other than Medina and Kufa / Bring your axes

I am not alone . . .

... وجهُ يافا طفلٌ / هل الشجَرُ الذابل يزهو ؟ هل تدخل
الأرض في صورة عذراء ؟ / مَن هناك يرجّ الشرقَ ؟ / جاء
العصف الجميل ولم يأت الخراب الجميل / صوتٌ شريدٌ . . .

خرجوا من الكتب العتيقة حيثُ يهتري‌ءُ الاصولْ
وأتوا كما تأتي الفصولْ
حضنَ الرمادُ نقيضَهُ
مشت الحقولُ إلي الحقولْ :
لا ، ليس من عصر الأفولْ
هو ساعة الهتْكِ العظيم أتتْ و خلخلةُ العقول

(بيروت ، ^ خريف ١٩٧٠)

. . . The face of Jaffa is a child / How can withered trees blossom?
Has the Earth taken on the image of a virgin? / Who is there to shake
the East? / The beautiful storm has come but not the beautiful
devastation / A fugitive voice . . .

They emerged from the ancient books
Where the fundamentals are rotting away
They came as seasons come
The ashes embraced their opposite
Fields walked toward fields:
No. Not from the age of the decline:
The time of dreadful agitation is at hand, the shaking loose of minds.

    (Beirut, 1970)

هذا هو اسمي

محمد

THIS IS MY NAME

ماحياً كل حكمةٍ /
هذه ناريَ /
لم تبقَ آيةٌ – دميَ الآيةُ /
هذا بدني /

دخلتُ إلى حوضك /
أَرضٌ تدور حوليَ أعضاؤك نيلٌ يجري /
طَفَوْنا ترسّبْنا / تقاطعت في دمي قطعَتْ صدركِ أمواجيَ
انهصرت لنبْدأ : نسيَ الحبُّ شفرةَ الليلِ / هل أصرخُ
أنَّ الطوفان يأتي ؟ / لنبْدأ : صرخةٌ تعرج المدينةَ والناسُ
مرايا تمشي / إذا عبَر الملحُ التقينا هل أنتِ ؟ /

[39]

Erasing every wisdom /
    This is my fire /
    No sign remained—My blood is the sign /
    This is my beginning /

I entered your enclosure /
    Earth revolving around me, your organs a Nile flowing / We drifted, we settled / You intersected my blood and my waves crossed your chest, you broke apart. Let us begin: Love forgot the blade-edge of night / Shall I scream that the flood is coming? / Let us begin: A scream scales the city and the people are mirrors walking / When the salt has crossed, we shall meet. Is it you?

– حبّيَ جرحٌ
جسَدي وردةٌ على الجرح لا يُقطفُ إلا موتاً . دمي
غُصُنٌ أسلم أوراقَه استقرّ ...

هل الصخرُ جوابٌ ؟ هل موتك السيدُ النائم يُغْوي ؟
عندي لثديك هالاتُ وَلوعٍ لوجهك الطفل وجهٌ مثلهُ ...
أنتِ ؟ لم أجدك
و هذا لهبي مَاحياً

دخلت إلى حوضك عندي مدينةٌ تحت أحزانَ
عندي ما يجعل الغُصُنَ الاخضرَ ‹ افعى› والشمسَ عاشقةً
سوداءَ عندي . . . /

[40]

—My love is a wound

My body a rose upon the wound, unpluckable except at death. My blood is a bough that surrendered its leaves and then settled down . . .

Is the stone an answer? Does your death, that sleeping master, beguile you? I have halos of craving for your breasts, for your child–like face a face like it . . .You? I did not find you

This is my flame which erases.

I entered your enclosure. Beneath my sorrows, I have a city, I have what makes vipers of the green branches, of the sun a black lover, I have . . ./

تقدَّموا فقراءَ الأرض غطّوا هذا الزّمان بأسمال
و دمْعٍ غطّوه بالجسد الباحث عن دفنه . . . المدينةُ
أقواسُ جُنونٍ / رأيتُ أن تلدَ الثورة أبناءها ، قبرت
ملايين الأغاني و جئتُ (هل أنت في قبريَ) ؟ هاتي ألمسْ
يديك اتبعيني زَمني لم يجىءْ و مقبرة العالم جاءت / عندي
لكلّ السلاطين رمادٌ / هاتي يديك اتبعيني . . .

قادرٌ ان أغيّر : لغمُ الحضارة – هذا هو اسمي

(لافتة)

Approach, you wretched of the earth, cover this age in rags and tears, cover it with a body searching for its warmth . . .The city is arcs of madness / I believed that the revolution bore its children. I buried millions of songs and I came. (Are you in my grave?) Come that I may touch your hands: Follow me. My time has not come but the graveyard of the world has / I have ashes for all the sultans / Give me your hands: Follow me . . .

I am able to transform: the land-mine of civilization— this is my name
  (a sign)

. . . وقفت خطوة الحياة على باب كتاب محوته
بسؤالاتيَ : ماذا أرى ؟ أرى ورقاً قيل استراحت فيه
الحضارات (هل تعرف ناراً تبكي ؟) أرى المئة اثنين
أرى المسجدَ الكنيسةَ سيّافيْن والأرض وردةً /

طار في وجهيَ
نَسرٌ / قدّستُ رائحة الفوضى / ليأت الوقتُ الحزين
لتستيقظ شعوب اللهيب والرفض / صحرائيَ تنمو /
أحببتُ صفصافةً تحتارُ بُرْجاً يتيهُ مئذنة تهرمُ
أحببتُ شارعاً صَفُّ لبنان عليه أمعاءَهُ في رسومٍ
و مرايا وفي تمائمَ /

[42]

. . . Life's footsteps stopped at the chapterdoor of a book erased by my questions. What do I see? I see pages in which they say civilizations rest. (Do you know a fire that weeps?) I see the hundred as two. I see mosque and church as two executioners and the earth as a rose /

An eagle
flies in my face / I have sanctified the scent of anarchy / Let the time of sorrow come, let the nations of flame and refusal awaken / My desert is growing / I loved a confused willow, a wandering tower, a decrepit minaret. I loved a street upon which Lebanon arrayed its entrails in pictures in mirrors in amulets /

قلتُ الآن أعطي نفسي لهاوية الجنس وأعطي للنار فاتحة
العالم قلتُ استَقرّ كالرمح يا نيرون في جبهة الخليقة روما
كلّ بيتٍ روما التخيّل والواقع روما مدينةُ الله والتاريخ
قلتُ استقرّ كالرمح يا نيرون ... /

لم آكل العشية غير الرّمْل ، جوعي يدورُ كالأرض
أحجارُ قصورٌ هياكلٌ أتهجّاها كخبزٍ / رأيت في دميَ
الثالث عينيْ مُسافرٍ مزج النّاس بأمواج حلمه الابديّ
حاملاً شعلةَ المسافات في عَقلٍ نبيّ، و في دمٍ وَحْشيٍّ /

[43]

I said I now give myself to the abyss of sexuality and give fire the conquest of the world. Settle down, Nero, I said, stuck like a javelin in the brow of Creation. Rome is every house, Nero, Rome is fantasy and reality, Rome is the city of God and History. Nero, I said, settle down like the javelin. Nero . . . /

I ate nothing but sand for supper, my hunger revolving like the earth stones, palaces, temples that I spell as bread / In my third blood I saw a traveler's eyes blending people with the waves of his eternal dream, carrying the torch of distances in prophetic knowledge in savage blood /

. . . وعليٌّ رموهُ في الجبّ غَطّوهُ بقَشٍّ والشمس تحمل
قتلاها وتمضي / هل يعرف الضوءُ في أرض عليّ طريقَهُ ؟
هل يلاقينا ؟ سمعنا دماً رأينا أنيناً /

سنقول الحقيقة : هذي بلادٌ
رفعت فخذَها
رايةٌ ...
سنقول الحقيقة : ليست بلاداً
هي إصطبلنا القمريّ
هي عُكازة السّلاطين سجّادةُ النبيّ

[44]

. . . And Ali, they threw him into the well and covered him with straw while the sun carried her dead and moved on / Does the light know its way in the land of Ali? Does it encounter us? We heard blood, saw wailing /

We shall speak the truth: This is a country
 Which raised its thighs
 As a banner . . .

We shall speak the truth: This is not a country,
 It is our lunar stable,
 It is the scepter of sultans,
 the prayer rug of the prophet.

سنقول البساطة : في الكون شيءٌ يسمّى الحضور وشيءٌ
يسمّى الغيابَ نقول الحقيقةَ :
نحن الغيابْ
لم تلدنا سماءٌ لم يلدنا ترابْ
إننا زبدٌ يتبخّرُ من نَهَر الكلمات
صدأٌ في السماء وأفلاكها صدأٌ في الحياة !
(منشور سرّي)

وطني فيٌّ لاجىءٌ
وليكنْ وجهيَ فيئاً !

[45]

We shall speak plainness: In existence there is something called
     presence, and something called absence. Let us speak truth:
     We are absence
     Sky did not beget us, dust did not beget us
We are a foam evaporating from rivers of words
Rust in the sky and its heavens, rust in life!
     (a coded message)

My homeland finds refuge in me.

Let my face be cast as a shadow.

دهرٌ من الحجَر العاشق يمشي حولي أنا العاشق الأول
للنار تحملُ النار أيّاميَ نارٌ أنثى دَمٌ تحت نهديها صليلٌ والإبط
آبارُ دَمع نَهرٌ تائهٌ وتلتصق الشمس عليها كالثوب تزلقُ /
جرحٌ فرّعتْه وشعشعَتْه بباه ٍ وبهار ٍ (هذا جنينُك ؟)
أحزانيَ وَردٌ

دخلتُ مدرسة العشب جبيني مُشقّقٌ ودمي يخلع
سلطانه ُ : تساءلتُ ما أفعلُ ؟ هل أحزم المدينة بالخبز ؟
تناثرتُ في رواق ٍ من النار / اقتسمْنا دَم الملوك وجعْنا

[46]

An eternity of ardent rocks encircles me, I am the first lover to the fire. The fire is pregnant: My days are female fire-blood: Beneath her breasts a rattle: the armpit a well of tears, a wandering river, the sun clinging to them like a dress slipping / A wound branching out and shining with potency and spice (Is this your fetus?) My sorrows are roses

I entered the school of grass. My forehead split open, my blood bereft of power. I asked myself: What should I do? Do I wall the city in with bread? I scattered myself in porticos of fire / We divided up the blood of the kings. We hungered.

نحمل الأزمنه
مازجين الحصى بالنجومْ
سائقين الغيومْ
كقطيعٍ من الأحصنَه

قادرٌ أن أغيّر : لغمُ الحضارة - هذا هو اسْمي

الأمّة استراحتْ
في عسل الرباب والمحرابْ
حصّنها الخالقُ مثلَ خندقٍ
وسدّهُ .

لا أحدٌ يعرفُ أين الباب
لا أحدٌ يسأل أين البابْ .

(منشور سرّي)

[47]

We carried the times
Blending pebbles with stars
Corralling the clouds
Like a herd of stallions

I am able to transform: the land-mine of civilization—this is my name

The nation found rest
In the honey of the rabab and the mihrab
The Creator fortified it like a trench
And barricaded it.

    No one knows where the door is
    No one asks where the door is.
              (a coded message)

... و عليّ رموهُ في الجبّ كان الجمر ثوباً له اشتعلنا تمسّكنا بأشلائه اشتعلتُ مساءَ الخير يا وردةَ الرّماد / عليّ وطنٌ ليس لإسمه لغة ينزف نفياً و يُثبت العشب والماء عليّ مهاجرٌ /

أين يغفو سيد الحزن كيف يحمل عينيه ؟ سمائي مخنوقةٌ كتفي تهبط و الأرض خوذةٌ مُلئتْ رملاً وقَشا هلعْتُ أركض غطّتني سُنونوةٌ نهضتُ لهيبٌ ناهداها نهضتُ أفتحُ شبّاكاً : حقولٌ خضرٌ أنا الفاتح الآخر والأرض لعبةٌ فرسٌ تدخل في الغيم /

يخرج الشجرُ العاشقُ غصنٌ يهزّني انْبجس الماءُ انتهى زمن الناس القديمُ ابتدأتُ وجهي مداراتٌ وفي الضوء ثورةٌ

[48]

. . . And Ali, they threw him into the well. The embers were for him a garment. We blazed, we clung to his remains. I blazed: Good evening, O rose of ashes. Ali is a homeland whose name has no language, bleeding negation, affirming the water and grass. Ali is an émigré /

Where does the master of sadness sleep? How does he carry his eyes? My sky is strangled, my shoulder sags and the earth is a helmet filled with sand and straw. Shuddering, I gallop. A swallow covers me. I rise. Its breasts are a flame. I rise. I open a window: Green fields . . . I am the Other Conqueror, and the Earth a game, a mare entering the clouds /

The loving trees leave, a branch shakes me. The water gushes, the time of ancient man has ended. I begin. My face is orbits and in the light is revolution

أيقظتْني قريةٌ في مهبّه / انكسِ الصمتُ احتضنّي
يا خالقَ التعب امنحني أراجيحكَ امتحنّي أنا الصخرة و البحث
و السؤالُ و لا عيدٌ و لا موقدٌ أنا الشبَح الراصدُ في فجوة
المدينة والناس نيامٌ / دخلتُ في شرَك الضوء نقياً كالعُنْف
أسطعُ كالتيه خفيفاً أطرافيَ البرق أطرافي رياحٌ منحوتةٌ /
ليس عظمي طعمَ تاج أو فضّةٍ لستُ مُلْكاً ودمي هجرةُ
السماء وعيناي طيورٌ / يُقال جلدكَ شوكٌ لتمتْ ولتكن
سمائيَ من جلدكَ صفراء قيل جلدك دهرٌ راسبٌ في قرارة
الحلم /

ولتُولدْ حرابُ الوقيعة الأبديّهْ
بيننا حفرة انهدام ٍ وصوتي
هذيانُ المغير يكسر عُكّاز الأغاني ويقلع الأبجديّهْ /

[49]

A village wakes me in the home of the wind. The silence broke / Embrace me, creator of fatigue, give me your hammocks, test me: I am the stone, the search, the question, where there is no festival, no hearth. I am the spectre, watchful in the openings of the city while the people sleep / I entered a trap of light, pure as violence, lightly I shone like pride, my limbs lightning, my limbs hewn winds / My bones do not have the taste of a crown or of silver. I am not property: My blood is the exodus of the sky and my eyes are birds / They say your skin is a thornbush: So die and let my skies turn yellow in your skin. They say your skin is eternity, silted in the bottom of the dream /

Let the spears of the eternal battle be born
There is a pit of destruction between us.
My voice is the ravings of the raider
As he shatters the scepter of songs and uproots the alphabet/

. . و النساءُ ارتحن في مَقصورةٍ
يستجرْنَ الكتبَ المستنزَلهْ
ويُحوكّن السماءْ
دميةً أو مقصلهْ
وعليّ فاتحٌ أحزانَه
لبهاليل الشقاء
للذين استنْسروا وانكسروا . .

وعليّ لهبٌ
ساحرٌ مشتعلٌ في كلّ ماءْ
عاصفاً يجتاحُ – لم يترك تراباً أو كتاباً
كَنس التاريخ غطّى
بجناحيه النهارْ
سرّه أنّ النهار
جُنّ /

. . . And the women relax in the private chamber
Invoking the Revealed Books
And transforming the sky into a doll or a guillotine
Ali opens his sorrows to the jesters of misery
To those who soar like eagles
And who were shattered . . .

Ali is a flame
A sorcerer ablaze in every water
Ravaging like a tempest—sparing neither dust nor book
Sweeping away history, covering
With his wings the daylight
Delighted that the day is
Crazed /

هذا زمنُ الموت ، ولكن
كل موتٍ فيه موتٌ عربيّ
تسقط الأيام في ساحاته
كجذوع الأرزة المكتهلهْ
إنه آخرُ ما غنّى به
طائرٌ في غابةٍ مشتعلهْ /

[51]

This is the time of death
And yet every death is an Arab death
The days collapsing in its courtyards
Like trunks of decayed cedar
It is the swansong of a
Bird in a burning forest /

وطني راكضٌ ورائي كنهرٍ من دمٍ / جبهة الحضارة قاعٌ
طحلبيٌّ / لملمت تاجاً تقمّصْتُ سراجاً / هامت دمشق حَنَّت
بغداد / سيفُ التاريخ يُكْسر في وجه بلادي / مَن الحريقُ
مَن الطوفانُ ؟ /

كنت الصحراء حين أسرتُ الثلجَ فيك انشطرتُ مثلك
رملاً وضباباً صرختُ أنت إلهٌ لأرى وجهه لأمحوَ ما يجمع
بيني و بينه قلتُ جاسدتك أنت الشقُّ المليءُ بأمواجي أنا
الليلُ حافياً حين أدخلتك في سُرّتي تناسلت في خطوي
طريقاً دخلت في مائيَ الطفل / استضيئي تأصّلي في متاهي

خدَرٌ مثمرٌ يعرّش حول الرأس حلمٌ تحت الوسادة أيّاميَ
ثقبٌ في جيبيَ اهترأ العالَمُ / حوّاءُ حاملٌ في سراويلي/
أمشي على جليد
ملذّاتيَ أمشي بين المحيّر والمعجز أمشي في وردةٍ /

My homeland gallops behind me, a river of blood / The brow of
civilization is the algae-crusted seabed / I mustered up a crown, I was
reincarnated as a lamp / Damascus wandered, yearning, Baghdad moaned,
longing / The sword of history is broken in the face of my country /
Who is the fire? Who the flood? /

You were the desert when I shackled the ice within you. Like
you, I split into sand and fog. And I scream you are a god, in order
to see his face, to erase what is between us. I said: I incorporated
you, you are a fault filled with my waves. I was the night, barefoot,
when I introduced you into my navel. You fathered my steps as a
road, you entered my waters in their infancy / Seek light, root
yourself firmly in my loss

A fruitful numbness trellises around my head: a dream beneath
the pillow: my days are a hole in my pocket: the world crumbles / Eve
is pregnant in my trousers /
    I walk upon the ice of my pleasures,
I walk between the perplexing and the miraculous, I walk in a rose /

زهرات اليأس تذوي

والحزن يصدأ / جيشٌ من وجوهٍ مسحوقةٍ يعبر التاريخ جيشٌ
كالخيط أسْلَمَ واستسلمَ ، جيشٌ كالظلّ / أركض في صوت
الضحايا وحدي على شفة الموت كقبرٍ يسيرُ في كرة الضوء .

انصهرنا

دَمُ الأحباء كالأهداب يحمي سمعتُ نبضك في جلدي (هل
أنت غابةٌ ؟) سقط الحاجزُ (هل كنت حاجزاً) ؟ سأل
النورس خيطاً في البحر يغزله الربّان غنّى ثلج المسافر شمساً
لا يراها (هل أنت شمسيَ ؟) شمسي ريشةٌ تشرب المدى/
سمع الضائع صوتاً (هل أنت صوتيَ ؟) صوتي زمني نبضك
الشهيّ ونهداك سوادي وكل ليلٍ بياضي
زحفت غيمةٌ فأسلمتُ للطوفان وجهي وتهتُ في أنقاضي ...

The flowers of
hopelessness wilt, and sorrow rusts. An army of pulverized faces
crosses history. An army, like thread, submits and surrenders, an
army like the shadows. I gallop in the voice of the victims, alone
on the brink of death, like a grave walking in a sphere of light

We are fused together.
The blood of the loved ones protects as eyelashes do. I heard your
pulse in my skin (are you a forest?) The obstacle fell (were you an
obstacle?) The seagull questioned a thread in the sea, woven by the
captain. The ice of the traveler chanted an invisible sun (are you
my sun?) My sun is a feather drinking space / The lost one heard a
voice (Are you my voice?) My voice is my time. Your inviting
pulse and your breasts are my darkness. And every night is my
whiteness.
A cloud crawled along: I surrendered my face to the flood and
wandered in my debris . . .

هكذا أحببتُ خيمه
وجعلت الرملَ في أهدابها
شجراً يمطر والصحراء غيمَهْ
قلتُ : هذي الجرّة المنكسره
أمّة مهزومة ، هذا الفضاءْ
رَمَدٌ . هذي العيونْ
حُفَرٌ . قلت الجنونْ
كوكبٌ مختبىءٌ في شجره .

سأرى وجه الغرابْ
في تقاطيع بلادي ، وأسمّي
كفناً هذا الكتابْ

[54]

That is how I loved a tent
How I made the sand in its eyelashes trees that rained
Made the desert a cloud
I said: This broken earthen pot
Is a vanquished nation, this space
A stye, these eyes
Pits. I said: madness is a
Planet concealed in a tree

I shall see the face of the raven
In the features of my country, and I shall call
This book a shroud

وأسمّي جيفةً هذي المدينه
وأسمّي شجرَ الشام عصافير حزينه
(ربما تولَدُ بعد التسميهْ
زهرة أو أغنيهْ)
وأسمّي قمرَ الصحراء نخلهْ
ربما استيقظت الأرض وعادت
طفلةً أو حلْم طفله

لم يعد شيءٌ يغنّي أغنياتي :
سيجيء الرافضونْ
و يجيء الضوء في ميعاده ...

لم يعد غيرُ الجنونْ

[55]

I shall call this city a cadaver
And I shall call Syria's trees mournful birds
(A flower or a song perhaps
Will be born of the naming)
And I shall call the desert moon a palm tree
Perhaps the earth shall awaken and become
A child again or the dream of a child

There is nothing left to sing my melodies:
        The dissenters shall come and
The light shall come at its appointed hour . . .

Only madness remains

هل لتاريخيَ َ في ليلكَ طفلٌ
يا رمادَ المدفأه
غضبُ الثورة جمرٌ عاشقٌ
و أغانيُّ امرأه :
هل لتاريخيَ َ في ليلكَ طفلٌ ؟ /

ألغبارُ التراثيّ في العظم / ألجأ ؟ هل يلجىءُ الغبارْ ؟
لا مكانٌ و لا ينفع الموتُ . . . هذا دُوارْ
من يرى جثة العصور على وجهه ويكبو   لا حراك
يحسّ الكهولةْ
حُلمةٌ للطفوله ْ .

قادرٌ أنْ أغيّر : لغمُ الحضارة – هذا هو اسمي

Is there in your nightfall a child for my history
O ashes of the hearth?
The anger of the revolution is ardent embers
And my songs are a woman:
Is there in your nightfall a child for my history? /

The legacied dust is in the bones / Shall I take refuge there? Does dust
give refuge? No place, and death is of no use. . . . This is the
dizziness of someone who sees the corpse of the ages on his face and
stumbles motionless
Someone who senses that
old age is a nipple for infants.

I am able to transform: the landmine of civilization—this is my name

عُدْ إلى كهفكَ التواريخُ أسرابُ جرادٍ ، هذا التاريخُ
يسكن في حضن بغيّ يجترّ يشهقُ في جوف أتانٍ ويشتهي
عفَنَ الأرض ويمشي في دودةٍ عُدْ إلى كهفكَ و اخفض
عينيك /

ألمح كِلمهْ

كلنا حولها سرابٌ وطينٌ لا امرؤ القيسَ هزّها والمعرّي
طفلُها وانحنى تحتها الجُنَيْدُ انحنى الحلّاج والنّفريّ / روى
المتنبّي أنه الصوت والصدى أنتَ مملوكٌ هيَ المالكُ ^/] انفصلْ
عن مسارات خطاها تَضع تغرُّب تصرْ غولاً تصرْ
مَسلخاً/ هي الحلمُ والحالمُ وهْيَ] الملاكُ/ [ترتسمُ الأمةُ] فيها
كبزرةٍ /
عُدْ إلى كهفكَ /

ماذا ؟ نَفوهُ أو قتلوهُ ؟ /

Return to your cave. Histories are swarms of locusts. This
history lives in the bosom of a whore, regurgitating, sobbing in the
belly of a she-ass, yearning for the rottenness of the earth, and
walking in a maggot. Return to your cave and lower your eyes /

I notice a word

Around it every one of us is a mirage, is clay. Imrul Qays did
not shake it. Ma'arri was its child. Junayd was huddled beneath it
And Hallaj and Niffari were huddled too / Mutanabbi related that it
was the voice and the echo* / You are the subject, it the sovereign /
Remove yourself from the paths of its steps and you are lost, alienated,
become a demon, a slaughterhouse / It is the dream, the dreamer, it
is the angel / The nation is sown in it like seed /

Return to your cave /

What? Did they banish him or did they kill him? /

---

*These are all major figures from the Arabic-Islamic tradition. All were icono-
clasts of one form or another.

قتلوهُ . . . لا لن أحدّث عن موت صديقي : ريفٌ من الزّهر الأصفر حولي / لكن سأكتب عن آخر غصنٍ في أرزة البيت عن رفّ يمامٍ يجرّ سجّادة الليل عن الحلم عالياً كبروجٍ / قتلوه لا لن أفوهَ بأسماء شهودٍ و قاتلينَ أو قاتلينَ و لن أبكي / سأبكي لأمةٍ ولدت خرساء للتمّ حاضناً زرقة الشطآن يبكي: لِمَ البكاء على طفلٍ على شاعرٍ ؟/ سأكتب عن آخر فيْءٍ لأرزة البيت عن رفّ حمامٍ يجرّ سجّادة الليل عن الحلم عالياً كجبالٍ /

وضعَ السيد الخليفة قانوناً من الماء شعبُه المرَقُ الطينُ سيوفٌ مصهورة ٌ وضع السيد تاجاً مُرصّعاً بعيون الناس/ هل هذه المدينة آيٌّ ؟ هل ثياب النساء من ورق المصحف / أدخلت محجري
في مضيقٍ حفرته الساعاتُ ساءلت هل شعبيَ نهرٌ بلا مصبّ ؟

[58]

They killed him . . . No, I shall not speak of the death of my
friend. A meadow of yellow flowers surrounds me / But I shall write
about the last branch of the familiar cedar, about the pattern of the
ringdoves' flight, hauling the carpet of night away from a dream,
high as towers / They killed him. No, I shall not utter the names of
the witnesses or of the murderers and I shall not weep / I shall weep
for a nation born mute, for a weeping swan hatching the blueness of
the shores: Why weep over a child, over a poet? / I shall write of the
last shadow of the familiar cedar, of the flight of doves, dragging the
carpet of night away from a dream, high as the mountains /

His eminence the Caliph issued a law made of water. Its people
are broth, clay, molten swords. His eminence wore a crown inlaid
with people's eyes / Is this city verses of Scripture? Are the women's
clothes pages from the Holy Book? /

I admitted my eye sockets into a mountain pass dug out
by the hours. I wondered: Are my people a river with no outlet?

أغنّي

لُغَة النصْل أصرخُ انثقب الدهر وطاحت جدرانُه بين
أحشائي تقيّأت لم يعد ليَ تاريخٌ ولا حاضرٌ / أنا الأرَقُ الشمسيّ
والفوهة الخطيئة والفعلُ انتظرني يا راكب الغيم أشيائيَ
تُغوي والشمس تخبط أطرافي أنا الساكن المدى والمزامير أنا
الغصنُ لاجئاً : إصْغِ هل تسمع هذا النواح في كبد العالم؟ /
أصغي للموت بين تجاعيدي / هَذَيْنا / هذيت كي أحسن الموت
اصطفيتُ النهدين بين تقاليديَ /

هل جلدك السقوط هل الفخذان
جرحٌ ملأتهُ / التأم العالم / هل أنت مقلعُ الليل في جلديَ ؟
فأسي مسنونةٌ صرتُ نبعاً آخراً ضفّتي تسيل ذراعاك اغترافٌ
قوسٌ حملتك وجهي صخَبٌ طائر تقاسَمهُ الصوت اسْأليني
أجبْ ... / تكلّم جَفْرٌ رصدتني خيولهُ انطفأ الهمسُ
(أعندي أعندك الآن ما يُهمس ؟) / نارٌ ملجومة سُفُنٌ
تجنَحُ بحرُ مروّض / فتح النورس عينيه أغلقي نسيَ الفتحة في
ريشه المشعّث ماءٌ وشرارٌ / لو كان لو عرف الرعد لو الرعد
في يديَّ /

هُدوءاً هذه قُبّة وسُكناىَ في فوهَة نهد / أظلّ أحفر
لو غيّرت لو غيّر الغبارُ عذاراه لو النارُ همزةٌ ... /

I sing
the language of the spearhead. I shout that time is punctured, that its
walls have crumbled in my bowels. I vomited: I have no History,
no present / I am Solar insomnia, the Abyss, Sin, and Action. Wait
for me, rider of the clouds. My possessions beguile: the sun strikes
my limbs. I dwell in the expanse and the psalms, I am the branches
in refuge. Listen: Do you hear this wailing in the heart of the
world? / I listen to death in my wrinkles / We raved / I raved in order
to die well. I selected two breasts from among my traditions /

Is your skin
the fall? Are your thighs a wound that I filled? / The world healed /
Are you the quarry of night in my skin? My pickaxe is sharpened, I
have become another spring, my bank overflows. Your arms reach
out and scoop it up: I carried you. My face is a clamor in flight, a
voice divided. Ask me and I shall reply . . . / It was Divination that
spoke: Its horses lay in wait for me, the whisper died down (Do I, do
you, now have something to whisper?) / Bridled fire, stranded ships,
pacified sea / The seagull opened its eyes—shut yours—and forgot
the gap in its ruffled feathers. Water and sparks / If only the thunder
was, if only it knew, if only it were in my hand . . . /

Calm down. This is a dome. My home is the summit of a
breast / I am still digging. Were I to change, were dust to change its
face, if fire were but a *hamza* . . .

ذُبْتُ في جنسيَ
جنسي بلا حدودٍ ولا سيف تلاشيْ لاشي تلاشيتُ وجهٌ
واحدٌ نحن لا قميصيَ تفّاحٌ ولَا أنت جنّة نحن حقل وحصادٌ
والشمس تحرسُ أنضجتُك جيئي من ذلك الطرف الأخضر هذا
قطافنا جسدانا زارع حاصدٌ / وحيدةَ أعضائيَ جيئي من ذلك
الطرَف / استحضرتُ موتي / وسلسليني ملكنا جَمْرةَ الوقت
والحنين ملكنا رَغَد الكون وهو يلتحف الناس اهتدينا . . . /

قرأتُ في ورقٍ
أصفرَ أنّي أموت نفياً تنوّرت الصحارى شعبي يشطّ َ . . . /
نبشنا كلماتٍ دفينة طعمها طعمُ العذارى / دمشق تدخل في
ثوبيَ خوفاً حبّاً تخالط أحشائيَ تلغو . . . /

لفظت جلدك خلّي شفتيك
اصهريهما بين أسناني أنا الليل والنهارُ أنا الوقتُ انصهرنا تأصّلي
في متاهي . . . /

[60]

You dissolved in my sexual pleasure, my frontierless,
swordless pleasure. Annihilate yourself, down to nothing. Nothing.
I annihilated myself. We are one face. My shirt is no apple and you
are no Eden. We are a field, a harvest, guarded by the sun. I ripened
you. Come from that green field edge. This is our yield: Our two
bodies are a sower, a reaper / Limb of mine, one and only, come from
that edge / I summoned up my death / Go through my entire history:
the live coal of time is ours. Longing is ours, the opulence of the
cosmos, wrapped in mankind, ours. We have found our way . . . /

                                              I read in pages
yellowing that I shall die in exile. I lit up the deserts: my people
stray . . . / We exhumed the buried words, flavored like virgins /
Damascus, in fear and in love, enters my garment, mixes with my
entrails, talks nonsense . . .

                          You sloughed off your skin; let your lips be,
let them melt between my teeth. I am night and day. I am time. We
have fused: Take root in my loss /

هكذا أحببتُ خيمه
وجعلتُ الرمل في أهدابها
شجراً يمطر والصحراء غيمه°
ورأيتُ اللّهَ كالشحّاذ في أرض عليّ
وأكلت الشمس في أرض عليّ
وخبزت المئذنه°
و رأيت البحر يأتي في ضباب المدخنه
هائجاً يهمس :
مَن كوّونا
لم يكن تكوينه إلا سقيفَه°
رجُها الإعصار فانهارت و صارت
خشباً يُحرَقُ في دار خليفه° .
نادرٌ أن ينطقَ البحرُ ولكن
نطقَ البحرُ : يبسنا
يبس التاريخ من تكراره
في طواحين الهواء
سقطَ الخالق في تابوته
سقطَ المخلوقُ في تابوته . . .

That is how I loved a tent
How I made the sand in its eyelashes trees that rained
Made the desert a cloud
I saw God as a beggar in the land of Ali
I ate of the sun in the land of Ali
I baked the minaret into bread
And I saw the sea unfurl in the mist of the smokestack, turbulent
Mumbling:

> Whoever fashioned us
> His fashioning was nothing more than a roofed shelter
> Shaken by the whirlwinds, demolished and then become
> Wood to be burned in the Caliph's house.

Seldom does the sea speak but

> It spoke thus: "We have dried up
> History has dried up from its own repetition
> In the windmills
> The Creator crumpled in his casket
> Creation crumpled in its casket . . ."

والنساء ارتحْن في مقصورةٍ
ينتشلن الليلَ من آباره
ويخيّطنَ السماءْ
ويغنّين : عليّ لهبٌ
ساحرٌ مشتعلٌ في كل ماءْ
ويسائلن السماء :
نجمةُ أو موميا
هذه الأرضُ ؟
ويفتقنَ السماء
ويرقّعن السماءْ

قبرَ الدجّالُ في عينيه شعباً
نَبش الدجّال من عينيه شعباً
وسمعناه يصلّي فوقَه
ورأيناه يحيّيه ويجثو
ورأينا
كيف صار الشعب في كفيه ماء
ورأينا
كيف صار الماء طاحونَ هواءْ /

And the women relax in the private chamber
Hoisting the night from its wells
Sewing the sky, singing:
"Ali is a flame,
    A magician ablaze in every water"
And they asked the sky:
"Is this land
A star or a mummy?"
And they unsewed the sky
And then patched it up

    Dajjal the Antichrist buried a people in his eyes
    Dajjal the Antichrist exhumed a people from his eyes
    And we heard him praying above them
    And we saw him bringing them to life and kneeling
    And we saw
    How the people became water in his palms
    And we saw
    How the water became a windmill /

جزرٌ للهيب تصعدُ فيها آسيا يصعدُ الغدُ انطفأت شمسٌ
حلمنا بغير ما هجسَ الليل / نهاري يقاسُ باللهب / استصرختُ
صوتُ الشعوب يفتتحُ الكونَ ويُغوي /

لستُ الرمادَ ولا الريحَ

سريري أشهى وأبعدُ / أقفاصُ دروبٌ مهجورةٌ فرس
الماضي رمادٌ وصبغةُ اللّه لونٌ آخرٌ /

لا يَدٌ عليّ

[63]

Islands made for flame, Asia rising in them, tomorrow rising in them. A sun was extinguished, we dreamed things that do not occur to the night / My day is measured by the flame / I cried for help, the voice of the people conquers the cosmos and beguiles /

I am neither the ashes nor the wind.

My bed is the most sensuous, the most distant / Cages, abandoned paths, horse of the past, are all ashes. And the tint of God is a different hue /

Not a hand over me.

عليّ أبدُ النار والطفولة / هل تسمع برق العصور تسمع
آهات خطاها ؟ هل الطريقُ كتابٌ أو يدٌ ؟ / إصبعُ الغبار
كدرويشٍ يغنّي ملكَ الأساطير / هاتوا وطناً قرّبوا المدائن
هزّوا شجر الحلم غيّروا شجر النوم كلامَ السماء للأرض /
طفلٌ تائه تحت سرّة امرأةٍ سوداء بحثاً
طفلٌ يشبّ
وللأرض إله أعمى يموت . . . /

سلامٌ

Ali is the eternity of the fire and of childhood / Do you hear the
lightning of the ages? Do you hear the sighs of their footsteps? Is
the path a book or a hand? / The fingers of dust are like a dervish
singing for the king of fables / Bring a homeland. Draw close the
cities. Shake the trees of dreams. Change the trees of sleep, the
colloquy of sky and Earth /

    A child lost beneath the navel of a black woman, searching
    A child who grows
    For the Earth, a blind god dies . . . /

Peace

لوجوهٍ تسير في وحدة الصحراء للشرق يلبس العشب والنارَ
سلامٌ للأرض يغسلها البحر سلامٌ لحبّها . . .

عُرُيكَ الصاعقُ أعطىَ
امطاره يتعاطانيَ رعدٌ في نهديَ اختمر الوقتُ تقدَّمُ هذا
دمي ألقُ الشرق اغترفْني و غبْ' أضعْني لفخذيك الدويّ
البرق اعترفني تبطُن جسدي / ناريَ التوجّه والكوكب جرحي
هدايةُ أُتهجَّى . . . /

[65]

To faces walking to the solitude of the desert to the East,
wearing grass and wearing fire. Peace to the Earth, washed by the
sea, peace to its love . . .

Your stark
nakedness proffered its rains to me. Thunder engulfs me. In my
chest time ferments. Advance. This then is my blood: the brilliance
of the East. Scoop me up and vanish, lose me. The echoing, the
lightning belong to your thighs. Scoop me up, cover yourself with
my body. My fire is the signpost and the star, my wound guidance.
I spell . . . /

أتهجّى نجمةً أرسمُها
هارباً من وطني في وطني
أتهجّى نجمةً يرسمها
في خطى ايامه المنهزمه
يا رماد الكلمه

هل لتاريخيَ في ليلك طفل ؟

لم يعد' غير الجنون'

[66]

I spell out a star which I draw
Fleeing from my homeland
In my homeland
I spell out a star which he draws
In the footsteps of his vanquished days
O ashes of the word

Is there in your night a child for my history?

Nothing but madness remains.

انني ألمحه الآن على شبّاك بيتي
ساهراً بين الحجار الساهره
مثل طفلٍ علمته الساحره
أنّ في البحر امرأه
حمَلتْ تاريخه في خاتمٍ
و ستأتي
حينما تخمد نارُ المدفأه
و يذوب الليل من احزانه
في رماد المدفأه . . . /

. . . ورأيت التاريخ في رايةٍ سوداءٍ يمشي كغابةٍ / لم أؤرِّخْ /

عائشٌ في الحنين في النار في الثورة في سحر سُمُّها الخلّاق
وطني هذه الشرارة ، هذا البرق في ظلمة الزمان الباقي . . .

(أوائل كانون الثاني ، ١٩٦٩)

[67]

I notice him now upon the windowsills of my house
Wakeful between the wakeful rocks
Like a child taught by a sorceress
That in the sea is a woman
Carrying his history in a seal-ring
That she shall come
When the fire of the hearth dies out
When the night has melted from its sorrows
In the ashes of the hearth . . . /

. . . And I saw History in a black banner, walking like a forest / I did
    not chronicle it /

I live in the longing, in the fire, in the revolution, in the witchery of its
    creative poison
My homeland is this spark, this lightning in the darkness of the time
    that remains . . .

(Early January, 1969)

قبر من اجل نيو يورك

مم

A GRAVE FOR

NEW YORK

I

حتى الآن ، تُرسم الأرض إجّاصةً
أعني ثدياً
لكن ، ليس بين الثدى والشاهدة إلا حيلةٌ هندسية :
نيو يورك ،
حضارة ﴿ بأربعة ﴾ أرجل كلّ جهة قتلٌ وطريق إلى القتل ،
وفي المسافات أنين الغرقى .

نيو يورك ،
امرأةٌ ــ تمثال امرأةٍ

في يدٍ ترفع خِرقةً يسمّيها الحرية ورقٌ نسمّيه
التاريخ وفي يدٍ تخنق طفلةً اسمها الأرض .

نيو يورك ،
جسدٌ بلون الإسفلت . حول خاصرتها زنّارٌ رطب ، وجهها

[71]

I

Until now, the Earth has been depicted in the shape of a pear
    by which I mean a breast
Yet, the difference between breast and tomb is a mere technicality:
    New York
A four-legged civilization; in every direction is murder or a road to murder
    and in the distance are the moans of the drowned.

New York,
A woman—the statue of a woman
    in one hand she holds a scrap to which the documents we call
    history give the name "liberty," and in the other she smothers
    a child whose name is Earth.

New York,
A body the color of asphalt. Around her waist is a damp girdle, her face

شبّاك مغلق ... قلت : يفتحه **وولت ويتمان** ــ « أقول
كلمة السر الاصلية » ــ لكن لم يسمعها غير الهِ لم يعد في
مكانه. السجناء ، العبيد ،[اليائسون]، اللصوص، المرضى
يتدفقون من حنجرته ، و لا فتحة ، لا طريق . و قلت :
جسر بروكلين! لكنه الجسر الذي يصل بين **ويتمان و وول
ستريت** ، بين الورقة ــ العشب و الورقة ــ الدولار ...

نيويورك ــ هارلم ،
من الآتي في مقصلة حرير ، من الذاهب في قبرٍ بطول
الهدسون ؟ انفجرْ يا طقص الدمع ، تلاحمي يا أشياء التعب .
زرقةٌ ، صفرةٌ ، وردٌ ، ياسمينٌ و الضوء يسنّ دبابيسه ،
و في الوجز تولد الشمس . هل اشتعلت أيها الجرح المختبىء
بين الفخذ و الفخذ هل جاءك طائر الموت وسمعت آخر
الحشرجة ؟ حبلٌ ، والعنق يجدل الكآبة و في الدم سويداء
الساعة ...

is a closed window . . . I said: Walt Whitman will open it—"I speak the password primeval"*—but no one hears it except an unreturning god. The prisoners, the slaves, the despairing, the thieves, the diseased spew from his throat.† There is no outlet, no path. And I said: "The Brooklyn Bridge!" But it's the bridge that connects Whitman to Wall Street, that connects leaves-grass to paper-dollars . . .

New York–Harlem,

Who comes in a guillotine of silk, who leaves in a grave the length of the Hudson? Explode, you ritual of tears. Cling together, you trifles of exhaustion. Blue, yellow, roses, jasmine: the light sharpens its points, and in the pinprick the sun is born. Have you ignited, O wound, concealed between thigh and thigh? Has the bird of death come to you and have you heard the death rattle? A rope, and the neck weaving melancholy; and in the blood, the melancholy of the Hour . . .

*"I speak the password primeval" is Walt Whitman, "Song of Myself," sect. xxiv, l. 10 (1872 ed.), which Adonis takes from Asselineau's translation, "Je profère le mot de passe des premiers âges." See Afterword, n. 27, present volume.

†This list is also from "Song of Myself," xxiv, 12–14: "Voices of the interminable generations of prisoners and slaves, / Voices of the diseas'd and despairing and of thieves and dwarves."

نيو يورك ـــ ماديسون ـــ بارك أفينيو ـــ هارلم ،

كسلٌ يشبه العمل ، عملٌ يشبه الكسل . القلوب محشوةٌ
إسفنجاً والايدي منفوخة قصباً . و من أكداس القذارة
وأقنعة **الامبايرستيت** ، يعلو التاريخ روائح تتدلّى صفائحَ
صفائح :

ليس البصر أعمى بل الرأس ،
ليس الكلام أجردَ بل اللسان .

نيو يورك ـــ وول ستريت ـــ الشارع ١٢٥ ـــ الشارع الخامس
سبحٌ ميدوزيٌ يرتفع بين الكتف والكتف . سوق العبيد من
كل جنس . بشرٌ يحيون ﴿كالنباتات﴾ في الحدائق الزجاجية .
بائسون غير منظورين يتغلغلون كالغبار في نسيج الفضاء ـــ
ضحايا لولبية ،

الشمس مأتمٌ
والنهار طبلٌ أسود .

[73]

New York–Madison–Park Avenue–Harlem,

Laziness resembling work, work resembling laziness. Hearts filled with
  sponge, hands swollen like reeds. And from the heaps of filth and the
  masks of the Empire State, History rises in odors suspended slab
  upon slab:

  It's not sight that is blind, rather the head,
  It's not speech that is barren, rather the tongue.

New York–Wall Street–125th Street–Fifth Avenue,

A Medusan specter ascends between the shoulders. A market with slaves
  of every race. Humanity living like plants in glass gardens. Unseen,
  Invisible wretches submerge like dust in the web of space spiraling
  victims:

  The sun is a funeral
  The day a black drum.

II

هنا ،

في الجهة الطحلبيّة من صجرة العالم ، لا يراني الا زنجيّ يكاد
أن يقتل أو عصفورٌ يكاد أن يموت ، فكّرت :
نبتةٌ تسكن في أصيصٍ أحمر كانت تتحول و أنا أبتعد عن
العتبة ، وقرأت :
عن فئران في بيروت وغيرها ترفل في حرير **بيت أبيض** ،
تتسلح بالورق وتقرض البشر ،
عن بقايا خنازير في بستان الابجدية تدوس الشعر ،

ورأيت :
أينما كنت ـ **بتسبورغ (أنتيرناشينال بويتري فورم) ،
جون هوبكنز (واشنطن)، هارفارد (كامبردج ،
بوسطن) ، آن آربر (ميشيغن ، ديترويت) ،
نادي الصحافة الاجنبية، النادي العربي في مقر
الامم المتحدة (نيو يورك) ، برنستون ، تمبل
(فيلادلفيا) ،**

II

Here,

On the mossy side of the Earth-rock, no one sees me but a black man
about to be killed or a sparrow about to die. I thought:
a plant living in a red claypot was being transformed as I distanced myself
from the threshold. And I read:
that rats in Beirut and elsewhere are strutting about in White House silk,
armed with documents and gnawing away at mankind, that
the remaining swine in the garden of the alphabet are trampling poetry.

And I saw

wherever I was—Pittsburgh (International Poetry Forum), Johns Hopkins
(Washington, D.C.),* Harvard (Cambridge; Boston), Ann Arbor
(Michigan; Detroit), The Foreign Press Club, The Arab Club at the
United Nations Headquarters (New York), Princeton, Temple
(Philadelphia)—

*Johns Hopkins's School of International Studies is in Washington D.C.

رأيتُ

الخريطة العربية فرساً تجرجر خطواتها و الزمن يتهدّل كالخرْج
نحو القبر أو نحو الظل الأكثر عتمة ، نحو النار المنطفئة
أو نحو نار تنتفئ ؛ تكتشف كيمياء البعد الآخر في
كركوك الظهران وما تبقّى من هذه القلاع في **أفراسيا**
العربية . وها هو العالم ينضج بين أيدينا . هَهْ ! نهيّء
الحرب الثالثة ، و نقيم المكاتب الأولى والثانية والثالثة
والرابعة لنتأكد :

١ – في تلك الناحية حفلة جاز ،

٢ ـ في هذا البيت شجصٌ لا يملك غير الحبر ،

٣ – في هذه الشجرة عصفور يغني ،

و لنعلن :

١ – الفضاء يقاس بالقفص أو بالجدار ،

٢ ـ الزمن يقاس بالحبل أو بالسوط ،

٣ – النظام الذي يبني العالم هو الذي يبدأ بقتل الأخ ،

٤ – القمر والشمس درهمان يلمعان تحت كرسي السلطان،

And I saw

the Arab map like a horse dragging its hooves and time drooping like a
saddlebag toward the grave or toward a darker shadow, toward the
dying fire or toward an extinguished fire; the chemistry of another
dimension is discovered in Kirkuk, in Dhahran, and is what remains
of such fortresses of Arab Afro-Asia. And here is the world ripening
in our hands. Ha! We prepare the Third World War, we set up the
First, Second, Third and Fourth Agencies to affirm that:

1. In that direction is a jazz party,
2. In this house is a man who owns nothing but ink,
3. In this tree is a bird that sings,

and to announce that:

1. Space is measured in units of cages or walls,
2. Time is measured in units of ropes or whips,
3. The régime that builds the world is the one that begins
   by killing its brother,
4. The sun and moon are two glittering dirhams beneath the
   Sultan's throne,

ورأيتُ
أسماء عربية في سعة الأرض أكثر حنوّاً من العين ، تُضيىء
لكن كما يضيئ كوكبٌ مشرّد «لا أسلاف له وفي خطواته
جذوره ... »

هنا ،

في الجهة الطحلبيّة من صخرة العالم أعرف ، أعترف . أذكر
نبتة ً أسميها الحياة أو بلادي َ، الموت َ أو بلادي ـــ ريحاً
تجمد كالملاءة ، وجهاً يقتل اللعب ، عيناً تطرد الضوء ،
وأبتكر ضدك يا بلادي ،

أهبط في جحيمك وأصرخ :
أقطّر لك ِ إكسيراً سامّا
و أحييك َ ،

و أعترف : نيويورك ، لك ِ في بلادي الرّواق والسرير ،
الكرسي والرأس . وكل شيء ٍ للبيع : النهار والليل ،
حجر مكة و ماء دجلة . وأعلن : مع ذلك تلهثين ـــ

and I saw,

Arab names as expansive as the earth, more compassionate than eyes,
shining but as a neglected star shines, "with no ancestors, and with
its roots in its steps . . ."*

Here,

On the mossy side of the Earth-rock, I know and I confess. I remember a
plant that I call life or my country, death or my country—a wind that
freezes like a mantle, a face that kills revelry, an eye that chases away the
light and I invent your opposite you, my country,

I sink into your hell and I scream out:
I distill a poisonous elixir for you
and I give you life,

and I confess: New York, in my country the curtain and the bed, the chair
and the head are yours. And everything is for sale: the day and the
night, the Black Stone of Mecca and the waters of the Tigris. I
announce: in spite of this you pant, racing in Palestine, in Hanoi, in

*The quotation is from Adonis's poem, "Knight of Strange Words: Psalm"
(Fāris al-Kalimāt al-Gharība: Mazmūr) from the collection *The Songs of Mihyar of
Damsacus (Aghānī Mihyār al-Dimashqī).*

تسابقين في **فلسطين** ، في **هانوي** ، في الشمال والجنوب ،
الشرق والغرب ، أشخاصاً لا تاريخ لهم غير النار ،
و أقول : منذ **يوحنا المعمدان** ، يحمل كل منا رأسه المقطوعَ
في صحنٍ وينتظر الولادة الثانية .

III

تفتّتي يا تماثيلَ الحرية ، أيتها المسامير المغروسة في الصدور
بحكمة تقلّد حكمة الورد . الريح تهبّ ثانية من الشرق ،
تقتلع الخيام وناطحات السحاب . وثمة جناحان يكتبان :
أبجديةٌ ثانية تطلعُ في تضاريس الغرب،
و الشمسُ ابنة شجرةٍ في بستان القدس .
هكذا أضرمُ لهبي . أبدأ من جديدٍ ، أشكّل وأحدّد :

نيو يورك ،
امرأةٌ من القشّ والسرير يتأرجَحُ بين الفراغ والفراغ،
وها هو السقف يهترئ : كل كلمةٍ إشارةُ سقوطٍ ،

the North and the South, in the East and the West, against people
  whose only history is fire,
and I say: ever since John the Baptist, everyone of us carries his severed
  head in a tray and awaits a second birth.

III

Crumble, you statues of liberty, you nails sunk into chests with a
  wisdom which counterfeits the wisdom of roses. The wind is raging
  again from the East, uprooting the tents and the skyscrapers. And
  there are two wings that write:
  a second alphabet rises from the undulations of the West,
  and the sun is the daughter of a tree in the garden of Jerusalem.

Thus do I light my flame. I begin anew, I fashion and I define:

  New York,
  a woman made of straw, the bed swinging from void to void, and
  overhead the ceiling is rotting: every word is a sign of a fall, every

كل حركةٍ رفشٌ أو فأس . وفي اليمين واليسار
أجسادٌ تحب أن تغير الحبُّ النظرَ السمع الشمُّ
اللمس والتغيّر ــ تفتح الزمن كبوّابةٍ تكسرها
وترتجل الساعات الباقية
الجنسَ الشعرَ الأخلاقَ العطشَ القولَ الصّمت
و تنفي الأقفال .

[و أغري بيروت وأخواتها العواصم ،
تقفز من سريرها و تغلق خلفها أبواب الذكرى . تدنو ،
تتعلّق بقصائدي، وتتدلّى. الفأس للرتاج والزهر للنافذة،
واحترقْ يا تاريخ الأقفال .]

قلت : أغري بيروت ،
ــ « ابحثْ عن الفعل . ماتت الكلمة »، يقول آخرون .
الكلمة ماتت لأن ألسنتكم تركت عادة الكلام إلى عادة المومأة.
الكلمة ؟ تريدون أن تكتشفوا نارها ؟ إذن ، اكتبوا .
أقول اكتبوا ، و لا اقول مَومِئوا ، و لا أقول انسخوا .

moment is a shovel or a pick.* And on the left and right are bodies
that want to change love sight hearing smell touch and change itself—
that open time like a portal that they then break,

and in the remaining hours improvise
sex poetry morals thirst speech silence
and negate the locks.†

And I tempt Beirut and her sister capitals,
They leap from their bed and close the doors of memory behind them.
They draw close, hanging from my odes, dangling. The pick is for
the gate, and the flowers for the window.
Burn, you history of locks.

I said: I tempt Beirut,
    —"Seek action. The Word is dead," the others say.
The word has died because your tongues have abandoned the habit of
speech for the habit of mime. The Word? Do you want to discover its
fire? Then, write. I say "write," I do not say "mimic," nor do I say "transcribe."

---

*This echoes Whitman, "Song of Myself," xxxiii, 132: "I heard the distant click
of their picks and shovels."

†This echoes Whitman, "Song of Myself," xxiv, 5–6: "Unscrew the locks from
the doors, / Unscrew the doors themsleves from their jambs."

اكتبوا — من المحيط إلى الخليج لا أسمع لساناً ، لا أقرأ كلمة . أسمع تصويتاً . لذلك لا ألمح من يلقي ناراً . الكلمة أخفّ شيء ، و تحمل كل شيء . الفعل جهةٌ و لحظةٌ ، والكلمة الجهات كلها الوقت كله.الكلمة — اليد، اليد — الحلم :

أكتشفك أيتها النار يا عاصمتي ،
أكتشفكَ أيها الشعر ،

وأغري بيروت . تلبسني و ألبسها . نشرد كالشعاع ونسأل : من يقرأ ، من يرى ؟ **الفانتوم** لدايان**والنفط** يجري إلى مستقرّه . صدق اللّه، ولم يخطئ **ماو** : « السلاح عاملٌ مهمّ جداً في الحرب ، لكنه غير حاسم . الإنسانُ ، لا السلاح ، هو العامل الحاسم » ، و ليس هناك نصرٌ نهائيٌّ و لا هزيمة نهائية . ردّدتُ هذه الأمثال والحكم ، كما يفعل العربي ، في **وول ستريت** ، حيث تصبّ أنهار الذهب من كل لونٍ آتيةً

Write—from the Ocean to the Gulf I do not hear a single tongue, I do not read a single word. All I hear is noise. Because of this I see no one throwing fire.

The Word is the lightest of things; and yet, it contains everything. Action is a direction and an instant, and the Word is all directions and all time. The Word—the hand, the hand—the dream:

I discover you O fire, O my capital,
I discover you O poetry,

and I tempt Beirut. She wears me and I wear her. We wander like rays and we ask: who reads, who sees? The Phantoms are for Dayan, and the Oil flows to its destination. God spoke true, and Mao wasn't mistaken: "Weapons are a very important factor in war, but they are not decisive. Men, not weapons are the decisive factor," and there is no such thing as final victory, nor is there total defeat.

I repeated these proverbs and maxims, as Arabs do, on Wall Street, where rivers of gold of every hue flow, coming from their sources. And I

من الينابيع . ورأيت بينها الأنهار العربية تحمل ملايين
الأشلاء ضحايا و تقدُمات إلى **الوثن السيد** . وبين الضحية
والضحية يقهقه البحارة فيما يتدحرجون من **كريزلر بيلدنغ**،
ليعودوا إلى الينابيع .

هكذا أضرم لهبي ،
نسكن في الصخب الاسود لتمتلئ رئاتنا بهواء التاريخ ،
نطلع في العيون السوداء المسيّجة كالمقابر لنغلب الكسوف،
نسافر في الرأس الأسود لنواكب الشمس الآتية .

IV

نيويورك ، أيتها المرأة الجالسة في قوس الريح ،
شكلاً أبعدَ من الذرّة ،
نقطة تهرول في فضاء الأرقام ،
فخذاً في السماء وفخذاً في الماء ،
قولي أين نجمعكِ ؟ المعركة آتية ٌ بين العشب والادمغة

saw among them Arab rivers bearing millions of corpses, victims and offerings to the Great Idol. And between the victims were sailors cackling as they rolled down the Chrysler Building, returning to their sources.

Thus do I light my flame,
> we live in a black clamor so that our lungs can be filled with the wind of History,
> we rise from black eyes hedged in like graveyards so that we can conquer the eclipse,
> we travel in the black head so that we can escort the coming sun.

IV

New York, woman seated in the arc of the wind,
> a body more remote than the atom,
> a point hurrying in the space of numbers.
> a thigh in the sky and a thigh in the water,
Say: where is your star? The battle between the grass and the computers

الالكترونية . ‹العصر› كله معلق على جدارٍ ، وها هو
النزيف . في الاعلى رأسٌ يجمع بين القطب والقطب ، في
الوسط آسيا ، وفي الاسفل قدمان لجسد غير منظور .
أعرفكِ أيتها الجثة السابحة في مسْك الخشخاش ، أعرفكِ
يا لعبة الثدى والثدى . أنظر إليكِ و أحلم بالثلج ، أنظر
إليكِ و أنتظر الخريف .

ثلجكِ يحمل الليل، ليلكِ يحمل الناس كالخفافيش ‹الميتة›. كل
جدارٍ فيكِ مقبرة . كل نهارٍ حفّارٌ أسود ،
يحمل رغيفاً أسودَ صحناً أسود
ويخطط بهما تاريخ **البيت الأبيض** :

ــ أ

ثمة كلابٌ تترابط كالقيد . ثمة قططٌ تلد خوذاً و سلاسل .
وفي الازقّة المتسللة على ظهور الجرذان ، يتناسل الحرس
الأبيض كالفطر .

is imminent. The whole epoch is suspended on a wall, and here is the
bleeding. Above, a head unites the two poles, at the waist is Asia, and
down below are two feet belonging to an unseen body. I know you, you
corpse swimming in the musk of poppies. I know you, you game of
breast upon breast: I look at you and I dream of snow, I look at you and I
await autumn.

Your snow carries the night, your night carries the people as dead bats.
    Every wall in you is a graveyard. Every day is a black gravedigger,
    carrying a black loaf, a black tray, etching
    with them the history of the White House:

(a)

    There are dogs lined up like links in a fetter. There are cats giving
    birth to helmets and chains. And in the alleyways that slink along
    the backs of rats, the white guards propagate like mushrooms.

‫ب -‬

امرأةٌ تتقدم وراء كلبها المسرج كالحصان . خطوات
الملك ، و حوله تزحف المدينة جيشاً من الدمع . وحيث
يتكدس الأطفال والشيوخ الذين يغطيهم الجلد الأسود ،
تنمو براءة الرصاص كالزرع ، ويضرب الهلع صدر المدينة.

‫ج -‬

هارلم ـ بدفورد ستويفنسنت : رملٌ من البشر يتكاثف
بروجاً بروجاً . وجوه تنسج الأزمنة . النفايات ولائم
للأطفال ، الأطفال ولائم للجرذان ... في العيد الدائم
لثالوثٍ آخر : الجابي، الشرطي، القاضي ـ سلطة
الفتك ، سيف الابادة .

‫د -‬

هارلم (الأسود يكره اليهودي) ،
هارلم (الأسود لا يحب العربي حين يذكر تجارة الرقيق) ،

(b)

A woman walking behind her dog bridled like a horse. The dog struts like
a king, as the city creeps around him like an army of tears. And where
the children and elderly, enveloped in a black skin, amass, the innocence
of bullets sprouts like a seed and terror strikes the heart of the city.

(c)

Harlem–Bedford–Stuyvesant: the sand of humanity thickens and piles up
in tower upon tower. Faces weave the times. The trash is a banquet for
the children and the children are a banquet for the rats . . . in the endless
feast is another trinity: the tax collector, the policeman, the judge—the
power of destruction, the sword of annihilation.

(d)

Harlem (the Blacks hate the Jews)
Harlem (the Blacks dislike the Arabs when they recall the slave trade),

هارلم — برودواي (البشر يدخلون كالرخويات في أنانبيق الكحول والمخدرات)

برودواي—هارلم ، مهرجان سلاسل وعصيّ ، والشرطة جرثومة الزمن . طلقةٌ واحدة ، عشر حمامات . العيون صناديق تتموّج بثلج أحمر ، والزمن عكاز يعرج . إلى التعب أيها الزنجيّ الشيخ ، الزنجي الطفل . إلى التعب أيضاً و أيضاً .

V

هارلم ،

لستُ آتياً من الخارج : أعرف ﴿حقدك﴾، أعرف خبزه الطيّب . ليس للمجاعة غير الرعد المفاجئ ، ليس للسجون غير صاعقة العنف .ألمح نارك تتقدم تحت الإسفلت في خراطيمَ وأقنعة ، في أكداسٍ من النفايات يحضنها عرش الهواء البارد ، في خطوات منبوذةٍ تَنْتَعِل تاريخ الريح .

Harlem Broadway (people infiltrate distillers of alcohol and drugs
like invertebrates)
Broadway Harlem, a festival of chains and sticks, and the police are
the germs of time. A single shot, ten pigeons. The eyes are boxes
surging with red snow and time is a crutch that hobbles. Onward, to
exhaustion, old Black man, young Black boy. To exhaustion, again
and again.

V

Harlem,
I do not come from outside: I know your hatred, I know its delicious
   bread. There is nothing but sudden thunder for famine, nothing for
   prisons but lightning bolts of violence. I notice your fire advancing
   beneath the asphalt in pipes and masks, in heaps of waste, embraced
   by the throne of the cold wind, in banished steps shod in the history
   of the wind.

هارلم،
الزمن يُحتَضر وأنتَ الساعة :
أسمع دموعاً تهدر كالبراكين ،
ألمح أشداقاً تأكل البشر كما نأكل الخبز .
أنت المحاة لتمحو وجه نيو يورك ،
أنت العاصفُ لتأخذها كالورقة وترميها .

نيويورك = SUBWAY + I.B.M. آتياً من الوحل والجريمة
ذاهباً إلى الوحل والجريمة

نيويورك = ثقباً في الغلاف الأرضي ينبجس منه الجنون
أنهاراً أنهاراً .

هارلم ، نيو يورك تُحتَضر وأنتَ الساعة .

VI

بين **هارلم** و **لنكولن سنتر** ،
أتقدم رقماً تائهاً في صحراء تغطيها أسنان فجرٍ أسود . لم يكن

Harlem,
Time is dying and you are the clock:

    I hear tears rumbling like volcanoes,
    I notice jaws eating mankind as they eat bread.
    You are the eraser with which to wipe away the face of New York,
    You are the storm that will seize it like a leaf and toss it away.

New York = I.B.M. + SUBWAY coming from mud and crime
    going to mud and crime.

New York = a perforation in the terrestrial covering from which gushes
    forth madness in river upon river.

Harlem, New York is dying and you are the clock.

VI

Between Harlem and Lincoln Center,
I proceed like a wandering number in a desert enveloped by the teeth of a

ثلج ، لم تكن ريح . كنت كمن يتبع شبحاً (ليس الوجه
وجهاً بل جرح أو دمع ، ليست القامة قامة بل وردة
يابسة) ، شبحاً ــ (هل هو امرأة ؟ رجل ؟ هل هو
امرأة ــ رجل ؟) يحمل في صدره أقواساً ويكمن للفضاء .
مرّت غزالة ناداها الأرض ، وظهر عصفور ناداه القمر .
وعرفت أنه يركض ليشهد بعث **الهندي الأحمر** ... في
فلسطين وأخواتها ،

والفضاء شريط رصاص ،
والأرض شاشة قتلى .

وشعرت أنني ذرةٌ تتموّج في كتلةٍ تتموج نحو الأفق الأفق
الأفق . وهبطت ‹ودياناً› تتطاول وتتوازى ، وخطر لي
أن أشكّ في استدارة الأرض ..

وفي البيت كانت **يارا** ،

يارا طرف أرضٍ ثانية و**نينار** طرفٌ آخر .
وضعتُ **نيويورك** بين قوسين وسرت في مدينة موازية .
قدماي تمتلئان بالشوارع، والسماء بحيرةٌ تسبح فيها أسماك
العين والظنّ وحيوانات الغيم . وكان **الهدسون** يرفرف

black dawn. There was no snow, there was no wind. I was like someone following a specter (the face is not a face but a wound, or tears, the figure not a figure but a dried-up rose), a specter—(is it a woman? a man? a woman-man?) carrying bows on his chest and ambushing space. A gazelle ran by, he called it Earth. A bird appeared, he called it Moon. And I realized that he was rushing to see the resurrection of the Red Indian . . . in Palestine and in its sister-lands,

> Space a ribbon of lead,
> The Earth a screen of murder.

And I felt as if I were an atom rippling in a mass itself flowing toward the horizon the horizon the horizon. And I descended into river valleys which run parallel and stretch on and on, and it occurred to me to doubt the roundness of the Earth . . .

And in the house was Yara,
Yara is the end of a second Earth and Ninar is the other end.
I placed New York between parentheses and walked in a parallel city. My feet filled with the streets, and the sky was a lake in which swam the of watchfulness and fancy and the animals of the clouds. And the

‹كغراب› يلبسُ جسد البلبل . وتقدّم نحوي الفجر طفلاً
يتأوه ويشير إلى جراحه . وناديت الليل فلم يجب . حمل
سريره واستسلم للرصيف . ثم رأيته يتغطى بريحٍ لم أجد
أرقّ منها غير الجدران و الأعمدة .. .. صرخة ، صرختان ،
ثلاث .. . و أجفلت نيويورك كضفدعٍ نصف جامد يقفز
في حوض بلا ماء .

لنكولن ،

تلك **هي نيويورك** : تتكئ على عكاز الشيخوخة وتتنزه في
حدائق الذاكرة ، و الأشياء كلها تميل إلى الزهر المصنوع .
و فيما أنظر إليكَ ، بين المرمر في واشنطن ، و أرى من
يشبهك في هارلم ، أفكر : متى تحين ثورتك الآتية ؟
ويعلو صوتي: حرّروا **لنكولن** من بياض المرمر، من **نيكسون،**
وكلاب الحراسة والصيد . أتركوا له ان يقرأ بعين جديدة
صاحب **الزنج علي بن محمد** ، وأن يقرأ الأفق الذي قرأه
ماركس ولينين و ماو تسي تونغ

والنَّفَري ، ذلك المجنون
السماويّ الذي أنْحلَ الأرضَ و سمح لها أن تسكن بين
الكلمة و الإشارة . و أن يقرأ ما كان يودّ أن يقرأه

Hudson was fluttering like a crow wearing the body of a nightingale. Dawn advanced toward me like a child groaning and pointing to his wounds. I called to the night but it did not answer. It carried its bed and surrendered to the sidewalk. Then I saw it enveloped in a wind exceeded in tenderness only by the walls and pillars. . . . A scream, two screams, three . . . and New York jumped up like a half-frozen frog leaping in a waterless pond.

Lincoln,
such is New York: leaning against a staff of old age and strolling in
    gardens of nostalgia, where everything inclines toward an artificial
    flower. And while I gaze at you, amidst all that marble in Washington,
    and see those who resemble you in Harlem, I wonder: when will
    your impending revolution come? And I raise my voice: Free
    Lincoln from the whiteness of marble, from Nixon, and from the
    watchdogs and hunting-dogs. Let him read with a new eye the leader
    of the Zanj, Ali ibn Muhammad, and let him read the horizon that
    Marx and Lenin and Mao Tse Tung read,
    and which al-Niffari
    read, that heavenly madman who made the world slight and permitted
    it to live between the word and the sign. And to read what Ho Chi

هوشي منه ، عروة بن الورد : « أقسّم جسمي في
جسومٍ كثيرةٍ ... » ، و لم يعرف عروة **بغداد** ، وربما
رفضَ أن يزور دمشق . بقي حيث الصحراء كتفٌ ثانية
تشاركه حمل الموت . وترك لمن يحب المستقبل جزءاً من
الشمس منقوعاً في دم غزالةٍ كان يناديها: حبيبتي ! واتفق
مع الأفق ليكون بيته الأخير .

لنكولن ،

تلك هي **نيو يورك**: مرآة لا تعكس إلا واشنطن . وهذه
واشنطن : مرآة تعكس وجهين ــ نيكسون وبكاءَ العالم.
ادخلْ في رقصة البكاء، انهضْ. ما يزال ثمة مكان، ما يزال
دورٌ ... أعشق رقصة البكاء الذي يتحول الى حمامةٍ
تتحول الى طوفان . « الأرض للطوفان محتاجة ... »

قلت البكاء وعنيت الغضب . عنيت كذلك الأسئلة : كيف
أقنع **المعرّة بأبي العلاء** ؟ سهولَ الفرات بالفرات ؟
كيف ﴿أستبدل﴾ الخوذة بالسنبلة؟(لابدّ من الجرأة لطرح أسئلة
أخرى على النبي والمصحف) ، أقول وألمح غيمةً تتقلد
النار ؛ أقول وألمح بشراً يسيلون كالدمع .

Minh had wished to read, ʿUrwa ibn al-Ward's: "I divide my body into many bodies . . ." ʿUrwa didn't know Baghdad, and refused to visit Damascus perhaps, remaining where the desert is a second shoulder, helping him to bear death. And he left to whomsoever loves the future a piece of the sun soaked in the blood of a gazelle he used to called "My beloved!" And he reached an agreement with the horizon to make it his last home.

Lincoln,

such is New York: a mirror that reflects nothing but Washington. And this is Washington: a mirror that reflects two images—Nixon, and the weeping of the world. Join the dance of the weeping, arise. There is still a place, there is still a role. . . . I love passionately the dance of the weeping that transforms into a dove that transforms into a flood. "The world is in need of a flood . . ."

I said weeping but I meant to say anger. I meant also the questions: How do I convince the village al-Maʿarra of the existence of Abul ʿAla? The banks of the Euphrates of the Euphrates? How do I replace the helmet with the spike of grain? (Courage is needed to submit other questions to the Prophet and to Scripture), I say and I notice clouds adorned with fire, I say and I notice people flowing like tears.

VII

نيو يورك ،

أحصرك بين الكلمة والكلمة . أقبض عليك ، أدحرجك ؛
أكتبك وأمحوك . حارّةً باردة ، بين بين . مستيقظة ،
نائمة ، بين بين . أجلس فوقك وأتنهد . أتقدمّك وأعلّمك
السير ورائي . سحقتك بعينيّ أنت المسحوقة بالرعب .
حاولت أن آمر شوارعك : استلقي بين فخذيّ لأمنحك
مدى آخر ؛ وأشياءك : اغتسلي لأعطيك أسماء جديدة .
كنت لا أجد فرقاً بين جسدٍ برأس يحمل أغصاناً نسميه
شجرة ، وجسدٍ برأس يحمل خيوطاً رفيعة نسميه انسانا ً.
واختلطت على الحجرة والسيارة، ويدا الحذاء في الواجهات
خوذةَ شرطي والرغيفُ صفيحة توتياء .

مع ذلك ، ليست **نيو يورك** لغواً بل كلمة . لكن حين
أكتب : **دمشق** ، لا أكتب كلمة بل أقلّد لغواً . دال ميم
شين قاف ... ما تزال صوتاً ، أعني شيئاً من الريح .
خرجت مرةً من الحبر ولم تعدْ . الزمن واقف حارساً
على العتبة يسأل:متى تعود، متى تدخل؟ كذلك بيروت
القاهرة بغداد لغوٌ شاملٌ كهباء الشمس ...

VII

New York,

I squeeze you between a word and a word. I grasp you and roll you; I
write you and erase you. Hot cold, in between. Awake asleep
in between. I crouch above you and I sigh. I walk in front of you and
teach you how to walk behind. I pulverized you with my eyes, you,
one pulverized with fright. I tried to command your streets: lie down
between my thighs so that I may grant you another dimension; and
your things: wash yourselves so that I may give you new names.

I could not see the difference between a body with a head bearing branches
that we call a tree, and a body with a head bearing fine threads that we
call a person. I confused a stone and a car, shoes in the shop-windows
appeared to me like a policeman's helmet, and a loaf like a sheet of
zinc.

In spite of this, New York is not nonsense, but a word. But when I write
Damascus, I do not write a word but rather I copy nonsense. D-a-m-
a-s-c-u-s . . . still just noise. I mean something of the wind that
flowed out of my ink once, never to return. Time stands guard at the
·threshold and asks: When will it return, when will it enter? Likewise
Beirut, Cairo, Baghdad are sheer nonsense like the fine dust of the
sun . . .

شمس ، شمسان ، ثلاث ، مئة ...

(استيقظ **فلانٌ** وفي عينيه اطمئنانٌ
يمتزج بالفلق . يترك زوجاته وأبناءه ويخرج حاملاً ببندقيته .
شمس ، شمسان ، ثلاث ، مئة ... ها هو كالخيط مهزوماً
ينزوي تحت نفسه . يجلس في المقهى . المقهى يمتلئ بحجارة
ودمىً نسميها رجالاً ، بضفادع تتقيأ الكلام وتوسخ المقاعد .
كيف يستطيع **فلانٌ** ان يثور وعقله مليئٌ بدمه ، و دمه مليئٌ
بالسلاسل ؟)

أسألك ، أنت من تقول لي :
أجهل العلم وأتخصّص بكيمياء العرب.

VIII

السيدةبروينغ، يونانية في **نيويورك.** بيتها صفحة من كتاب
المتوسط ــ الشرق . **ميرين ، نعمة الله ، ايف بونّفوا** ...
وأنا كمن يضيع ويقول اشياء لا تقال . كانت **القاهرة** تتناثر
بيننا ورداً يجهل الأزمنة ، وكانت **الاسكندرية** تختلط بصوت
كفافي وسيفيريس . « هذه أيقونة بيزنطية ... » ، قالت
والزمن يلتصق على شفتيها عطراً أحمر.كان الوقت يحدودب

a sun, two suns, three, a hundred . . .

(So-and-so gets up, in
his eyes tranquility mixed with anxiety. He quits his wives and his
children and leaves carrying a rifle. A sun, two suns, three, a hundred . . .
here he is like a thread, defeated, huddling within himself. He sits in a
coffee shop. The coffee shop is filled with stones and pawns we call men,
with frogs vomiting speech and soiling the seats. How can so-and-so
rebel when his mind is filled with blood and his blood is filled with
chains?)

I ask you, you who say to me:
I know nothing of science and yet
I specialize in the alchemy of the Arabs.

VIII

Mrs. Brewing, a Greek woman in New York. Her house is a page from
the book of the Mediterranean. Mirène, Niʿmatallah, Yves
Bonnefoy. . . . And me, like someone wasting away, mumbling
unspoken things. Cairo was scattered among us, like roses unaware
of the time, and Alexandria blended with the voices of Cavafy and
Seferis. "This is a Byzantine icon . . ." she said, as time clung to her

والثلج يتكئ ، (منتصف ليلة ٦ نيسان ١٩٧١)

ونهضت في الصباح صارخاً

قبيل ساعة العودة : **نيويورك !**

تمزجين الأطفال بالثلج وتصنعين كعكة

العصر . صوتك إكسيدٌ ، سمٌّ بما بعد الكيمياء ، واسمك

الأرقُ والاختناق .**سنترال بارك** تولم لضحاياها ، وتحت

الشجر أشباه جثث وخناجر . ليس للريح غير الأغصان

العارية ، ليس للمسافر إلا طريق مسدود .

ونهضت في الصباح صارخاً:**نيكسون**، كم طفلاً قتلت اليوم؟

ـ «لا أهمية لهذه المسألة ! » (**كالي**)

ـ « صحيح أن هذه مشكلة . لكن أليس صحيحاً كذلك

أن هذا ينقص عدد العدو ؟ » (**جنرال أميركي**)

كيف أعطي لقلب **نيو يورك** حجماً آخر ؟ هل القلب هو

كذلك يوسِّع حدوده ؟

نيويورك ــ جنرال موتورز الموت ،

« سنستبدل الرجال بالنار ! » (**مكنمارا**) ــ يجفّفون

lips like red perfume. Time was stooping, and the snow leaning
(midnight, April 6, 1971)

And in the morning I woke up screaming,
a little before the hour of my return: New York!

You mix the children with snow and you make cake
of the ages. Your voice is oxide, a poison beyond chemistry draws away,
and your name is insomnia and suffocation. Central Park gives a banquet
for its victims, and beneath the trees appear specters of corpses and
daggers. All that is left for the wind are naked branches, for the
traveler a blocked path.

And in the morning I woke up screaming: Nixon, how many children
    have you killed today?
    —"This matter is of no importance!" (Calley)

    —"It's true that this is a problem. But is it not also true that this
reduces the number of the enemy?" (an American General)

How can I give the heart of New York another expanse? Can the heart
    also expand its boundaries?

New York—General Motors death,
    "We shall replace men with fire!" (McNamara)—they dry the sea in

البحر الذي يسبح فيه الثوار ، و «حيث يجعلون من الأرض صحراء ، يسمون ذلك سلاماً ! » (**تاسيت**) .
ونهضت قبل الصباح ، وأيقظت **ويتمان** .

IX

وولت ويتمان ،
ألمح رسائل إليك تتطاير فس شوارع **منهاتن** . كل رسالةٍ عربةٌ ملأى بالقطط والكلاب . للقطط والكلاب القرن الواحد والعشرون ، وللبشر الإبادة :
هذا هو العصر الأميركي !

ويتمان ،
لم أرك في **منهاتن** ورأيتُ كل شيء . القمر قشرة تقذف من النوافذ ، والشمس برتقالة كهربائية . و حين قفز من **هارلم** طريق أسود في استدارة قمرٍ يتوكأ على أهدابه ، كان وراء الطريق ضوءٌ يتبعثر على مدى الاسفلت ، ويغور كالزرع بعد ان يصل إلى **غرينيش فيليج** ، ذلك الحي اللاتيني الآخر ، أعني الكلمة التي تصل إليها بعد أن نأخذ كلمةُ حبّ و تضع نقطة تحت الحاء . (اذكر انني كتبت

which swim the revolutionaries and "where they make the earth a
desert and call it peace!" (Tacitus).

I rose up before dawn, and woke up Whitman.

IX

Walt Whitman,
I notice letters to you flying in the streets of Manhattan. Every letter is a
  wagon full of cats and dogs. To the cats and dogs belong the
  twenty-first century and to man belongs annihilation:
  This is the American age!

Whitman,
I did not see you in Manhattan and yet I saw everything. The moon is a
  rind flung out the window, and the sun an electric orange. And when
  a black road, round like a moon reclining on its eyelashes, jumped up
  from Harlem, a light behind the road scattered over the extent of the
  asphalt, and sunk in like rooting seeds as it reached Greenwich
  Village, that other Latin Quarter, I mean the word that you get after
  you take the word *hubb* and put a dot beneath the *h*.* (I remember

Hubb means "love." A dot beneath the first letter gives *jubb*, "cistern."

ذلك في مطعم فايسروي بلندن ، ولم يكن معي غير الحبر.
وكان الليل ينمو كزغب العصافير) .

ويتمان ،

« الساعة تعلن الوقت » (**نيويورك** ـ المرأة قمامة ، والقمامة
زمنٌ يتجه إلى الرماد)

« الساعة تعلن الوقت » (**نيو يورك** ـ النظام **بافلوف** ،
والناس كلاب التجارب ... حيث الحرب
الحرب الحرب !)

«الساعة تعلن الوقت» (رسالة آتية من الشرق.طفل كتبها بشريانه.
اقرأها : الدمية لم تعد حمامة . الدمية
مدفع ، رشاش ، بندقية ... جثثٌ في
طرقات من الضوء تصل بين **هانوي**
والقدس ، بين **القدس والنيل .**)

ويتمان ،

«الساعة تعلن الوقت» وأنا
«أرى ما لم تره وأعرف ما لم تعرفه» ،

أتحرك في مساحة شاسعة من علبٍ
تتجاور كسراطين صفراء في محيطٍ

writing that in London's Viceroy Restaurant, when all I had was ink.
And the night was growing like down on a bird).

Whitman,
"The clock indicates the moment"* (New York–woman is garbage, and
    garbage is time heading toward ashes)
"The clock indicates the moment" (New York—The conditioning is
    Pavlovian, the people are the experimental dogs . . . where
    there is war, war, war!)
"The clock indicates the moment" (a letter coming from the East.
    A child wrote it with his arteries. I read it: the doll is no
    longer a dove. The doll is a cannon, a machine gun, a
    rifle . . . corpses in roads of light connecting Hanoi and
    Jerusalem, Jerusalem and the Nile.)

Whitman,
"The clock indicates the moment" and I,
"I see what you did not see, I know what you did not know,"
    I move in a vast expanse of tin cans that cluster
    around one another like yellow crabs in an ocean of

---

*"The clock indicates the moment" is Whitman, "Song of Myself," xliv, 10.
The Arabic is closer to the French: "L'horloge indique l'heure."

من ملايين الجزر — الأشخاص ؛ كل
واحدة عمود بيدين وقدمين و رأس
مكسور . وانتَ
« أيها المجرم ، المنفيّ ، المهاجر »
لم تعد إلا قبّعةً تلبسها عصافير لا تعرفها
سماء اميركا !
ويتمان ، ليكنْ دورُنا الآن . أصنع من نظراتي سلّماً . انسج
خطواتي وسادةً ، وسوف تنتظر . الإنسان يموت ، لكنه
أبقى من القبر . ليكن دورنا ، الآن . أنتظر ان يجري
الفولغا بين **منهاتن وكوينز** . أنتظر ان يصب **هوانغ هو**
حيث يصب **الهدسون**. تستغرب ؟ ألم يكن **العاصي يصبّ
في التيبر** ؟ ليكن دورنا الآن . أسمع رجّةً وقصفاً .
وول ستريت وهارلم يلتقيان — يلتقي الورق والرعد ،
الغبار والعصف. ليكن دورنا، الآن . المحار بيني أعشاشه
في موج التاريخ . الشجرة تعرف اسمها . وثمة ثقوب في
جلد العالم ، شمسٌ يغيّر القناع والنهاية وتنتحب في عين
سوداء . ليكن دورنا ، الآن . نقدر ان ندور أسرع
من الدولاب ، ان نحطّم الذرة ونسبح في دماغ إلكتروني
باهت او متلألئ ، فارغ او مليئ ، وان نتخذ من العصفور

millions of people–islands; each a
pillar with two hands, two feet,
and a severed head. And you
"you criminal, you exile, you emigrant"*
are nothing but a hat worn by birds unknown
to the American sky.

Whitman, let it be our turn now. I make a ladder of my gaze. I weave
my steps into a pillow, and we shall wait. Man dies but he is more
eternal than the grave. Let it be our turn now. I wait for the Volga
to flow between Manhattan and Queens. I wait for the Hwang Ho to
empty where the Hudson empties. Are you surprised? Did the
Orontes not flow into the Tiber? Let it be our turn now. I hear a
convulsion and a roar of thunder. Wall Street and Harlem meet—leaves
meet the thunder, dust meets the tempest. Let it be our turn now.
Oysters build their nests in the wave of history. The tree knows its
name. And there are perforations in the skin of the world. A sun
changes masks and the ending, and weeps in a black eye. Let it be our
turn now. We can turn faster than the wheel, split the atom and
swim in an electronic brain that is pale or shimmering, empty or full,
and make birds a homeland. Let it be our turn now. There is a little

*Whitman, "The Sleepers," i, 44: "The emigrant and the exile, the criminal
that stood in the box."

وطناً. ليكن دورنا ، الآن . ثمة كتاب احمر صغير يصعد .
لا الخشبةُ التي اهترأت تحت الكلمات بل هذه التي تتسع
وتنمو ، خشبة الجنون الحكيم ، والمطر الذي يصحو لكي
يرث الشمس . ليكن دورنا ، الآن . **نيويورك** صخرة
تتدحرج فوق جبين العالم . صوتها في ثيابكَ و ثيابي ،
فحمها يصبغ اطرافك واطرافي ... استطيع ان أرى
النهاية ، لكن كيف اقنع الزمن لكي يبقيني حتى أرى ؟
ليكن دورنا ، [لنرفع الفأس] الآن . وليسبح الزمن في
ماء هذه المعادلة :

نيويورك + **نيويورك** = القبر أو أي شيء٬ بجيء٬ من القبر
نيويورك − **نيويورك** = الشمس

X

في الثمانين أبدأ الثامنة عشرة . قلت هذا أقول وأكرّر ولم
تسمع بيروت .
جثةٌ هذه التي توحّد بين البشَرة والثوب
جثةٌ هذه المستلقية كتاباً لا حبراً
جثةٌ هذه التي لا تسكن في صرف الجسد و نحوِه

red book rising: not the stage crumbling to pieces beneath the words
but this one that expands and grows, a stage of wise madness and rain
that clears so that it can inherit the sun. Let it be our turn now.
New York is a rock that rolls on the forehead of the world. Its voice
is in your garments and in mine, its coal-blackness stains your limbs
and mine. I am able to see the end, but how can I convince Time to
spare me so that I may see. Let it be our turn, let us raise the pick,
now. And let Time swim in the water of this equation:

New York + New York = the grave or whatever comes from the grave
New York - New York = the sun.

X

In my eighties I shall begin again at eighteen. I said this repeatedly but
    Beirut does not hear.

A corpse this, which confuses the flesh for the garment
A corpse this, reclined as a book not as ink
A corpse this, which does not live in the morphology of the body nor
    in its grammar

جثةٌ هذه التي تقرأ الأرض حجراً لا نهراً
(نعم أحب الامثال والحكمة ، احياناً :

ان لم تكن مهيّماً ، تكن جثة !)

اقول و اكرر ،

شعري شجرة وليس بين الغصن والغصن ، الورقة والورقة الا
امومةُ الجذع .

اقول و اكرر ،

الشعر وردة الرياح . لا الريح ، بل المهبّ ، لا الدورة بل
المدار . هكذا ابطل **القاعدة** ، واقيم لكل لحظة قاعدة .
هكذا اقترب ولا اخرج . اخرج و لا اعود . واتجه نحو
أيلول و الموج .

هكذا ،

احمل **كوبا** على كتفيّ وأسأل في **نيو يورك**: متى يصل **كاسترو**؟
وبين **القاهرة** و **دمشق** أنتظر على الطريق المؤدي ...
...التقى غيفارا بالحرية . تغلغل معها
في فراش الزمن و ناما . و حين

A corpse this, which reads the Earth as stone not as river
    (Yes, I love proverbs and truisms, sometimes:
    if you do not know passion, you are a corpse!)

I say and I repeat,
    my poetry is a tree and there is nothing between branch and branch,
    between leaf and leaf except the motherhood of the trunk.

I say and I repeat,
    poetry is rose of the wind. Not the wind, but where the wind blows,
    not the rotation but the orbit. Thus do I invalidate rules, and
    establish a rule for every moment. Thus do I draw near and do not
    leave. I leave and do not return. And I head toward September, and
    the waves.

Thus,
Do I carry Cuba on my shoulders and ask in New York: when does
Castro arrive? And between Cairo and Damascus I wait on the road that
leads . . .

    . . . Guevara met with freedom. He sank with
    it in its bed of time and they slept. And when

استيقظ لم يجدها . ترك النوم
ودخل في الحلم ،
في **بيركيلي** ، في **بيروت الخلايا** ، حيث يتهيأ كل شيء
ليصير كل شيء .

هكذا ،
بين وجهٍ يميل الى **الماريجوانا** تحمل شاشة الليل ،
و وجهٍ يميل الى **الآي بي إم** تحمله شمس باردة ،
أجريت لبنان نهراً من الغضب ، و طلع **جبران** في ضفة وطلع
ادونيس في الضفة الثانية .
وخرجت من **نيويورك**، كما أخرج من سرير:
المرأة نجمة مطفأة والسرير ينكسر ،
اشجاراً بلا فضاء ،
هواءٌ يعرج ،
صليباً لا يتذكر الشوك .

والآن ،
في عربة الماء الاول، عربة الصور التي تجرح **ارسطو وديكارت**
أتوزع بين **الاشرفية ومكتبة رأس بيروت**، بين **زهرة الاحسان**

he awoke he did not find it. Abandoning
    sleep, he entered the dream,
in Berkeley, in Beirut and the remainder of the cells, where everything is
    ready to become everything.

Thus,
between one side that inclines toward marijuana borne by the screen of
night, and one side that inclines toward IBM borne by a cold sun,
I cause Lebanon to flow as a river of anger, Gibran rising on one bank,
    Adonis on the other.
And I left New York, as I leave my bed:
The woman is an extinguished star and the bed breaks
a tree without space,
a crippled wind,
a cross that does not remember the thorn.

And now,
in a carriage of first water, a carriage of pictures that wound Aristotle
and Descartes, I scatter myself between Ashrafiyya and the Raʾs Beirut

ومطبعة **حايك وكمال** ، حيث تتحول الكتابة الى نخلة والنخلة
الى يمامة
حيث تتناسل **الف ليلة وليلة** وتختفي **بثينة وليلى**
حيث يسافر **جميل** بين الحجر والحجر ، وما من أحد يحظى
بقيس .

لكن ،
سلامٌ لوردة الظلام والرمل
سلامٌ **لبيروت** .

(نيو يورك ٢٥ آذار ـــ بكفيا ١٥ ايار ١٩٧١)

Bookstore, between Zahratul Ihsan and the Hayek and Kamal Press, where writing transforms into a palm tree and the palm tree transforms into a dove

where the Thousand and One Nights multiply, where Buthayna and Layla vanish, where Jamil travels between stone and stone, and where not a soul finds Qays

But,
Peace to the rose of darkness and sand
Peace to Beirut.

(New York, March 25–Bikfayya, May 15, 1971)

AFTERWORD

Shawkat M. Toorawa

AFTERWORD

Shawkat M. Toorawa

Adonis is the pen name of ʿAlī Aḥmad Saʿīd.[1] He was born in 1930 in the village of Qassabin in Syria. In 1950, after schooling in Latakia, he entered the Syrian University in Damascus where he read literature and philosophy and where he came under the influence of the politician Anṭun Saʿāda. After brief imprisonment he left for Beirut with his wife, the critic Khālida Saʿīd, where they became naturalized as Lebanese citizens in 1956. The following year Adonis and fellow poet Yūsuf al-Khāl launched the avant-garde poetry journal, *Shiʿr* [Poetry] and founded the publishing house Dār Majalla Shiʿr. In 1968 Adonis founded his own journal, *Mawāqif* [Stations], like *Shiʿr* a forum for experimental and progressive poetry and literary opinion.

In 1973 Adonis completed his doctorate on the Arabic literary and critical tradition at St. Joseph's University of Beirut. Since then, he has taught at St Joseph's, the University of Geneva, Damascus University, the Sorbonne Nouvelle, and Georgetown University. He divides his time between Beirut, which he left at the height of the Lebanese Civil War, and Paris, although a number of year-long fellowships have recently taken him also to Princeton University and to the Institute for Advance Study in Berlin.

Adonis, who has been a Nobel finalist more than once, has received countless awards and honors, among them the Syria-Lebanon Award of the International Poetry Forum (Pittsburgh, 1971); the National Poetry Prize (Lebanon, 1974); the Grand Prix des Bienniales Internationales de la Poésie (Liège, 1986); the Nazim Hikmet Prize (Istanbul, 1994); and the Lerici-Pea Prize (Italy, 2000). In 1997, the French Government decorated Adonis Commandeur de l'Ordre des Arts et des Lettres.

✍

When Adonis first published *Waqt bayna al-ramād wa al-ward* [*A Time Between Ashes and Roses*] in 1970 under the imprint of his still new journal *Mawāqif,* the Arabic literary world was taken by surprise. The collection consisted of just two poems, "Introduction to the History of the Petty Kings," and "This Is My Name," introspective indictments of the failure of Arab culture, of Arab intellectuals, and especially of Arab leaders, to come to terms with both Western ascendance and the political landscape after Israel's military and political defeat of the Arabs in the 1967 war.

In 1972, Adonis issued an enlarged version of the collection, including a third poem, "A Grave for New York," one he began writing in the United States.[2] If the literary world had been taken by surprise in 1970, in 1972 it was stunned. The new poem was, like the first two, a political one, but it was also a work that engaged in a sophisticated and sustained dialogue with New York City and with Walt Whitman. Although Adonis had produced six important collections before *A Time Between Ashes and Roses* and has published ten more since, this volume remains central to understanding Adonis's poetic vision and his political and cultural commitments.

The purpose of this Afterword is neither to encapsulate that vision—the poems do that after all—nor to analyze the commitments or the poems themselves. Rather, I wish to offer the reader some insights that may contribute to an appreciation of what Adonis is trying to accomplish in *A Time Between Ashes and Roses.*

≥

One of the earliest collections of pre-Islamic poetry is an anthology entitled the *Mu'allaqāt,* comprising seven *qaṣīda*s (odes)—the number varies according to collection and collation—by poets who represent the more illustrious examples of the genre; the most famous of these poets is Imrul Qays (who makes an appearance in *A Time Between Ashes and Roses*). The *qaṣīda,* often fifty or more lines, was generally tripartite, and was in one rhyme and one meter.[3] Each line was a discrete unit, relying neither on the preceding nor the following one for complete meaning. Enjambement was therefore virtually impossible, the two-part (hemistich) nature of the line encouraging the juxtaposition of opposing or contrasting elements.

These stringent requirements, which *grosso modo* remained normative for fourteen centuries, were seen by many modern poets as stifling. Although the twentieth century Iraqi poets Nāzik al-Malāʾika and Badr Shākir al-Sayyāb were the first successful exponents of free verse in Arabic, breaking with the imposed rigidity of the classical ode and its meters and often deriving inspiration from the poetry of other languages and traditions, it is in Adonis's poetry that the break from conventional forms, the foray into experimental ones, and creative recourse to other world poetic traditions found its greatest expression. Adonis has called this the "New Poetry," *al-shi'r al-jadīd,* which is a conscious attempt to salvage from the past the forgotten and the common and make them new. Instead of simply discarding the canonical classical Arabic meters, for example, he reworks them, creating new ones, and new variations. Instead of the break between the two halves of the classical line, for instance, Adonis uses slashes, blank spaces and "etceteras."

"Perhaps the best way to describe New Poetry," Adonis wrote in 1959, "is to call it vision ($ru^{\circ}y\bar{a}$), by its very nature a leap outside existing comprehensions."[4] For Adonis, exemplars of that vision include members of the Mahjar movement, the Arab writers who emigrated to the Americas in the mid-nineteenth and early twentieth centuries, figures such as Mikhā'īl Nuʿaymah, Amīn al-Riḥānī, and the perennial Kahlil Gibran (Jubrān Khalīl Jubrān). Adonis associates himself with the doyen of this group in the closing stanzas of "A Grave for New York":[5] "Gibran rises on one riverbank, and Adonis rises on the other" (p. 96).[6] This new vision consists in a radical reconsideration of Arab and Arabic culture. In a celebrated paper delivered at a conference in Rome in 1961 and later published in *Zaman al-shiʿr* [The time of poetry] Adonis wrote that the Arab poet has for centuries lived in a closed world, unable to make sense of the future, that progress in that system consists always in turning or returning to the past.[7] For Adonis, the poet must not only quiz the past but, in order to do so, must himself emanate from it; he must be "a flame coming from an old fire," and at the same time something new, "something which differs totally from the old."[8] This is evident in the opening to "This Is My Name," a passage reprised several times in the poem in a kind of litany:

Erasing every wisdom /
    This is my fire /
        No sign remained . . . My blood is the sign /
        This is my beginning /

The new fire and the new flames are *words*:

Everything comes to the earth through the eye of a word: vermin, God, the poet, by puncturing and by insomnia and by feverish voice, by bullets and ritual ablutions . . .

("Introduction to the History of Petty Kings," 29)

And there are two wings that write: "a second alphabet rises from the undulations of the West"

("A Grave for New York," 77).[9]

For Adonis, "The word in poetry must transcend its essence, it must swell and include more than usual": words become "wombs with a new fertility [*raḥim li-khiṣb jadīd*]."[10] Adonis forces himself, and us, to seek in them not surface meanings but inner and universal truths.

Adonis is not only critical of succumbing to the weight of the stultifying and stultified past, but also of what he regards as Islam's theologies of political and artistic control. His three-volume *al-Thābit wa al-mutaḥawwil* [The static and the changing], completed in the 1970s, and revised in four volumes in 1994, includes a controversial and wide-ranging analysis of Islam and its legacies. But if Adonis is critical of the Islamic tradition, he is not cramped by it. His incorporation, adaptation, and recasting of Islamic motifs and symbols is informed by a deep knowledge of them. The tenth-century mystic, al-Niffarī, for instance, is one of the most important influences on him. Al-Niffarī figures in a number of Adonis's poems, including "This Is My Name" and "A Grave for New York," and Adonis named his journal *Mawāqif* for al-Niffarī's work, *Kitāb al-Mawāqif wa al-mukhāṭabāt* [The book of stations and speeches].[11] Another symbol, pervasive in Adonis's poetry, is ʿAli. This is ʿAli ibn Abī Ṭālib, cousin and son-in-law of the prophet Muḥammad, an early and vigorous convert, the fourth caliph (656–661) of Islam, the person to whom the prophet Muḥammad vouchsafed *bāṭinī* or esoteric knowledge, the one whom God favored with divinatory abilities, and the most important figure in the Shiʿite world view. But ʿAli is someone else too: ʿAlī Aḥmad Saʿid— Adonis himself (raised, incidentally, in an ʿAlawī Shiʿite family):

> . . . And Ali, they threw him into the well. The embers were for him a garment. We blazed, we clung to his remains. I blazed: Good evening, O rose of ashes. Ali is a homeland whose name has no language, bleeding negation, affirming the water and grass. Ali is an émigré/
>
> ("This Is My Name," 48)

Adonis's resonant use of traditional symbols of the Arab, Arabic, and Islamic literary and religious past has sometimes led to the banning of his works (e.g., [The static and the changing]) and to charges of heresy.

> . . . We carry God like a dying shaykh, we open to the sun a path other than minarets, to the child a book other than angels, to the dreamer an eye other than Medina and Kufa / Bring your axes
>
> ("Introduction to the History of the Petty Kings," 34)

To these charges Adonis responds that "paradoxically, the present-day victims of such accusations are—as were yesteryear's victims—the best preservers of the very same Arab cultural heritage in the name of which they are being condemned."[12]

The Near Eastern is another tradition of which Adonis sees himself a part, to be reworked, to be sure, but nonetheless integral. This explains his pen name, that of the Tammuzian Near Eastern god of the harvest who annually dies and annually rises. Adonis writes himself, and names himself, into the larger Near Eastern tableau: "The Arabs are themselves a Semitic people. They belong spiritually and intellectually to and with other Semitic peoples, such as the Arameans, the Phoenicians, and so on."[13]

The "and so on" keeps implicit something Adonis made explicit in 1993 when he attended a UNESCO-sponsored meeting in Granada also attended by a number of Israelis. In January 1995, Adonis was expelled from the Damascus-based Arab Writers' Union for this participation. Two prominent Syrian writers, in addition to publicly opposing the expulsion, which was carried by a majority vote, consequently resigned from the Union: the writer Ḥannā Mīna, and the playwright Saʿdallāh Wannūs. Like Adonis, Wannūs wrote devastating critiques in the aftermaths of 1967 and 1973 and, like Adonis, insisted on placing the blame and responsibility—and on locating the salve and the solution—in the Arab-Islamic world itself:

Let it be our turn now. We can turn faster than the wheel, split the atom and swim in an electronic brain that is pale or shimmering, empty or full, and make birds a homeland. Let it be our turn now.

("A Grave for New York," 93)

ﻙ

Adonis shares with his wife, the critic Khālida Saʿid, the conviction that one of the abiding questions for all Arab poets is how they can share seriously and deeply not only Arab culture, but with world culture. One strategy, the one Adonis has chosen, is to seek authenticity and validity in his own heritage, not as a refuge, or origin, but as a point of departure. This strategy involves making new *(al-tajdīd)*, questioning *(al-tasāʾul)*, and transformation *(al-taghyīr)*. Transformation is the subject of some of Adonis's most memorable images. In "Introduction to the History of the Petty Kings," we read:

In which the word is transformed into a web whose mesh is riddled with holes like carded cotton (29)

and in "This Is My Name":

. . . And the women relax in the private Chamber
Invoking the Revealed Books
And transforming the sky into a doll or a guillotine (50)

Transformation is also part of a chorus in "This Is My Name":

I am able to transform: the land-mine of civilization . . . this is my name
(a sign)

(41 and *passim*)

In the preface to the 1998 revised and enlarged edition of the collection of essays, *Fātiḥa li-nihāyāt al-qarn* [Preface to the century's endings], Adonis's closing sentiment reads: "Let this book's new edition, then . . . be a hand extended toward the many other hands which are igniting the flames of transformation."[14]

٭

As the reader of the *A Time Between Ashes and Roses* can attest, whether in English or in Arabic, the language is cryptic and enticing, and the images are arresting, now baffling and introspective, now patent and obvious. References, images, and quotations can be obscure and rooted in Adonis's poetic memory, or evident and manifest and part of the reader's realm of assumed experience. These are not the prose poems Adonis expounded upon in the early 1960s but the vers libre and free verse he would advocate in the 1970s. Among the more prominent Western practitioners of this free(d) verse are Rimbaud; Whitman; St.-John Perse, the complete works of whom Adonis has translated; and T. S. Eliot, whose writings, both theoretical and creative, have had a considerable influence on the course of modern Arabic poetry, and with whom Adonis has often been compared.[15]

Adonis's poetry also resonates his readings of Bonnefoy, Cavafy, and notably Baudelaire whom he mentions repeatedly in his critical works. Adonis has said that the genius of Baudelaire (and Mallarmé) finds its roots in the American tradition and owes a large debt to Edgar Allan Poe. No wonder then that it is in this tradition too that the poems of *A Time Between Ashes and Roses* find antecedents. In fact, the poems of *A Time Between Ashes and Roses* are, like Eliot's *The Wasteland* and William Carlos Williams' *Paterson,* "long poems": new experiments with poetry as a public language, "celebrations of the city, models for good government, values and visions by which to live."[16] And no wonder their similarity to Whitman's poetry too.

Indeed, if Whitman's *Leaves of Grass* "could not possibly have emerged or been fashion'd or completed, from any other era"[17] than as his "young nation, irrepressibly vital and bitterly divided against itself, approach[ed] and then surviv[ed] the terrible bloodletting of the Civil War,"[18] so too was Adonis's collection shaped by the events leading up to 1967, when a similarly politically young region had to taste defeat against Israel and its allies. In the same way that Whitman did so for America and Americans, Adonis set out to write the poetry of the Arabs in the Arabic language, to sing the song of himself, his nation and his unloosed century, rejecting conventional literary themes, stock ornamentation, romance, rhyme, and formulation[19]. *A Time Between Ashes and Roses* is an invective and a corrective in the face of the impotence of the Arab world, of the ascendance of the West in general and America in particular, and of the world's ineffective and colonializing political systems.

In the dedication to "Introduction to the History of the Petty

Kings," Adonis greets Gamal Abdel Nasser: "the first modern Arab leader who worked to bring an end to the age of the Petty Kings and to begin another age." In *Falsafat al-thawra* [Philosophy of the revolution], Nasser wrote about the circumstances of history that have united the Arab world, of a community with many spiritual centers, from Mecca to Kufa, from Baghdad to Cairo. We hear resonances throughout the poems of *A Time Between Ashes and Roses*.[20] The refrain "in a map that extends . . . etc.," for instance, is Adonis's reforging of Nasser's promise to work so that the Arab homeland stretches from the Atlantic to the Arab Gulf.

For Adonis, Nasser's pan-Arab ideas of a unified Arab world may not have found fruition, but he did try to bring about something "new," and he was instrumental in the creation of a cohesive and united, if not unified, Third World. Adonis, too, is an advocate of a sort of pan-Arabism. He wants to see a unified Arab world, one capable of fighting the hegemony of the West, industrial imperialism, colonialism, zionism, and its anti-Arab sentiment and successes, and capable of fighting dissolution and monarchichal pettiness.

The magic of your history has ended
Bury its servile face and doltish inheritance

How did knowledge transform into shackles?
Is this why history refuses my face
Why I no longer see an Arab sun on the horizon?

When things turn serious, al-Andalus seeks the help of the pious king in saving the Peninsula, fallen into the hands of the Spaniards. He is content with apologies and condolences and says that war has its ups and downs and you should be content with a quick recovery.

("Introduction to the History of the Petty Kings," 31)

Adonis turns to history in this poem, specifically that of Islamic Spain and the fragmentation and infighting of its cities, to re-teach his fellow Arabs the lessons it has already so ruthlessly taught.

✿

Like Whitman, Baudelaire, Cavafy, Lorca, and others, Adonis is a poet of the city. The city is a recurrent theme, the subject of memorable images, and the axis around which are centered both "A Grave for New York" and "Introduction to the History of the Petty Kings." The opening line of "Introduction to the History of the Petty Kings" is: "The Face of Jaffa is a child" (7) and that of "A Grave for New York":

New York,
A woman, the statue of a woman
in one hand she holds a scrap which the documents we call history give the name "liberty," and in the other she smothers a child whose name is Earth. (71)[21]

Like his American counterparts, Adonis has asserted that poetry is linked to public life.[22] It is to their public that the Modernists speak, in poetry that is a collection of seemingly unremarkable experiences.[23] And it is these experiences, often very alien to critics and readers, that have often prompted them to assess the poems of *A Time Between Ashes and Roses* in harsh terms, leveling accusations of obscurantism, confusion and formlessness.[24] But it is through these very experiences that Adonis eternally questions the Arab-Islamic vision of everything, even the act of writing *(kitāba)* itself [25]. Adonis wants to give things new names, uncover them, ask questions, walk in a parallel dimension, forge and fashion, discover, realize, arrive, say, see, read, and change. These are the verbs of Whitman too. "A Grave for New York" is in effect a supreme acknowledgment of Whitman,[26] who makes his first appearance early in the poem:

New York,
A body the color of asphalt. Around her waist is a damp girdle,
her face is a closed window

I said: Walt Whitman will open it? "I speak the password primeval"
but no one hears it except an unreturning god. The prisoners, the
slaves, the despairing, the thieves, the diseased spew from his
throat. There is no outlet, no path. And I said: The Brooklyn
Bridge! But it's the bridge that connects Whitman to Wall Street,
that connects leaves-grass to paper-dollars . . .

(71–72)

This passage includes direct quotes from Whitman:[27]

I speak the pass-word primeval . . .
[. . .]
Through me many long dumb voices
Voices of the interminable generations of prisoners and slaves.
Voices of the diseas'd and despairing and of thieves and dwarfs

("Song of Myself," sect. xxiv, lines 12, 13–15)[28]

In 1980, Adonis published a revised edition of the collection *A Time Between Ashes and Roses* under the title *This Is My Name,* for what he evidently now regarded as the title poem; he also dispensed with the slashes so prominent in the 1972 rescension. "This Is My Name," completed in 1969, the year before Adonis wrote the more hopeful "Introduction to the History of the Petty Kings," is a devastating indictment on the Arab defeat in the 1967 war. It is, in poet-critic Salma Jayyusi's words, a poem "in which the drama of defeat is portrayed in sophistic, oblique terms, and the present and past mutilated beyond repair."[29] She goes on to write that Adonis's quest has been "to arrive at a mythic sense of race, and to root modern experience in a continuous history stemming from basic (according to him) repetitive equivalents in the past." She calls this elusive thing for which he searches a common denominator for Arab existence. In this poem, Adonis is at his most eloquent in showing that the less appealing aspects of Arab history ought to serve as examples from which the modern Arab can learn not to make the mistakes of his and her ancestors and predecessors.

My homeland gallops behind me, a river of blood / The brow of civilization is the algae-crusted seabed / I mustered up a crown, I was reincarnated as a lamp / Damascus wandered, yearning, Baghdad moaned, longing / The sword of history is broken in the face of my country / Who is the fire? Who the flood? /

("This Is My Name," 52)

"This Is My Name" may in fact be the pinnacle of Adonis's attempts to create the "total poem":

I call the "total poem" a poem which ceases to be merely an emotional moment, but becomes a global moment in which various types of expressions, prose or metrical, narrative or dialogue, singing, epic and fiction are integrated and in which consequently the intuitions of philosophy, science and religion embrace each other. The new poem is not only a new form of expression but also a form of existence.[30]

Adonis's poem becomes like Barthes's text of bliss, one that imposes a state of loss, that discomforts and "unsettles the reader's historical, cultural, psychological assumptions, the consistency of his tastes, values, memories, brings to a crisis his relation with language."[31] The poem becomes, ultimately, in Adonis's words, "a civilizational fabric, an open texture or web, in which both the rhythm of the self and the rhythm of the world commingle, embracing the creative cultural theme."[32]

Adonis's wife, a leading critic of modern Arabic literature, writes:

This poem marks the destruction of the principle of poetic stability, of methodology, of classicism. It proclaims the canon of change: every single poem must transcend all previous successes in poetry, including those of the poet himself. Each poem will then become a new land to be added to the known world. Thus, there can be no relaxation, no pause for breath, no final form, instead, continuous, ever-renewing creativity, unending risks bursting forth.[33]

She is describing "This Is My Name" but might be describing any of the three poems in *A Time Between Ashes and Roses*.

The historian Basim Musallam has noted, and asked: "The great paradox of Arab culture . . . is that whilst the common language and heritage of Arabic confer a veneer of unity and identity, the same factors—language and heritage—bequeath a legacy of particularism. The poet speaks for his tribe, his princely patron, his nation; but who speaks for all the Arabs?"[34]. I would like to close by suggesting that, perhaps, Adonis does:

I live in the longing, in the fire, in the revolution, in the witchery of its
        creative poison / My
homeland is this spark, this lightning in the darkness of the time
        that remains . . .

("This Is My Name," 67)

NOTES

1. The best biography of Adonis is Anne Wade Minkowski, "Biographie d'Adonis," in *Adonis. Un poète dans le monde d'aujoud'hui, 1950–2000* (Paris: Institut du monde arabe, 2000), 202–86. See also Stefan Weidner, "Adonis," in *Kritisches Lexicon zur fremdsprachigen Gegenwartsliteratur,* ed. Heinz Ludwig Arnold (Munich: Edition Text und Kritik, 1996), 1–11. For biographical details in English, see Shawkat M. Toorawa, "Adonis," in *Reference Guide to World Literature. Vol. 1: Authors,* 3d ed., ed. Sara and Tom Pendergast (Detroit: St. James Press, 2002), 6–9. See also Adonis's autobiography: *Hā-anta, ayyuhā al-waqt: sīra shiʿriyya thaqāfiyya* (Beirut: Dār al-Ādāb, 1993). Also useful are two conversations with Adonis: *al-Turāth wa al-thaqāfa al-waṭaniyya: naṣṣ ḥiwār al-shāʿir Adūnīs maʿa ʿAbd al-Fattāḥ Ismāʿīl* (Beirut: Dār Ibn Khaldūn, 1986), and Ṣaqr Abū Fakhr's *Ḥiwār maʿa Adūnīs: al-ṭufūla, al-shiʿr, al-manfā* (Beirut: al-Muʾassasa al-ʿArabiyya li al-Dirāsāt wa al-Nashr, 2000).

2. *Waqt bayna al-ramād wa al-ward* (Beirut: Dār al-ʿAwda, 1972), viz. the edition that forms the basis of the present volume. For details about the publication history of *A Time Between Ashes and Roses,* see Appendix B. "A Grave for New York" has received more translation attention than the other two poems, both in English (see the Bibliography) and in other languages; e.g., in Spanish: *Epitafio para Nueva York— Marrakech/Fez,* trans. Federico Arbós (Madrid: Hiperión, 1987), 21–51; and in Turkish, *Newyorkʿa mezar,* trans. Özdemir Ince (Istanbul: Varlık Yayınları, 1989). To the best of my knowledge, the only complete translation of the entire collection so far is into French: *Tombeau pour New York,* suivi de *Prologue à l'histoire des rois des tâʾifa* et de *Ceci est mon nom,* trans. Anne Wade Minkowski (Paris: Editions Sindbad, 1986; reprint: Actes Sud/Sindbad, 1999).

3. For details about the *qaṣīda* form, and for an excellent discussion of Arabic literature in general, see Roger Allen, *The Arabic Literary Heritage: The Development of Its Genres and Criticism* (Cambridge: Cambridge Univ. Press, 1998), which contains a useful guide to further reading at pages 407–16. For a taste of the first eight hundred years of Arabic literature, see *Night and Horses and the Desert: An Anthology of Classical Arab Literature,* trans. Robert Irwin (London: Allen Lane, 1999; New York: Anchor Books, 2000).

4. Adonis, *Zaman al-shiʿr* (Beirut: Dār al-ʿAwda, 1972), 9. As with most of his works, Adonis produced a revised edition of *Zaman al-shiʿr,* which appeared in 1978.

5. In addition to collaborating with Anne Wade Minkowski on a translation of Gibran's *al-Mawākib* into French as *Le Livre des Processions* (Paris: Arfuyen, 1998),

Adonis has also written the preface to the translation into French of *The Prophet,* Gibran's celebrated English work: *Le Prophète,* trans. Anne Wade Minkowski (Paris: Gallimard, 1992).

6. Pagination is that of the 1972 edition reproduced in this volume on facing pages (see note 2 above).

7. Adonis, *Zaman al-shiʿr,* 47–49.

8. Adonis, "Fātiḥa li-nihāyāt al-qarn," *Mawāqif* 36 (1980): 338. This essay appeared the same year in a volume of the same name, revised and enlarged in 1998. See note 14.

9. The phrase "second alphabet" would become the title of Adonis's 1994 collection, *Abjadiyya thāniya* (Casablanca: Dār Tūbqāl li al-Nashr, 1994), analyzed by ʿAbd al-ʿAziz Būmashūlī in *al-Shiʿr wa al-taʾwīl: qirāʿa fi shiʿr Adūnīs* (Casablanca: Afrīqiyā al-Sharq, 1998). Būmashūlī also analyzes Adonis's *al-Kitāb* [The book], which receives extensive treatment in Usayma Darwīsh, *Taḥrīr al-maʿnā: dirāsa naqdiyya fi dīwān Adūnīs: al-Kitāb I* (Beirut: Dār al-Ādāb, 1997). The late 1990s witnessed a flurry of publications on Adonis, in particular in French (see Bibliography), and in Arabic, e.g., ʿAdnān Ḥusayn Qāsim, *al-Ibdāʿ wa maṣādiruhu al-thaqāfiyya ʿinda Adūnīs* (Cairo: al-Dār al-ʿArabiyya li al-Nashr wa al-Tawzīʿ, 2000), and Wāʾil Ghālī, *al-Shiʿr wa al-fikr: Adūnīs namūdhajan* (Cairo: al-Hayʾa al-Miṣriyya al-ʿĀmma li al-Kitāb, 2001).

10. Adonis, *Zaman al-shiʿr,* 17.

11. Adonis wrote the Afterword ("Vers une étrangeté familière,") to the most recent French translation of this work, *Le livre des stations de Niffarī,* trans. Maati Kabbal (Sommières: Editions de l'éclat, 1989), 163-170. He has also written a book on Islamic mysticism entitled *al-Ṣūfiyya wa al-sūriyāliya* [Sufism and surrealism] (Beirut: Dār al-Sāqī, 1992). The most recent study of Adonis and Sufism is Khālid Balqāsim, *Adūnīs wa al-khiṭāb al-Ṣūfī* (Casablanca: Dār Tūbqāl li al-Nashr, 2000).

12. This (new) phrasing is from the French essay, "Le poète arabe contemporain face à l'héritage (1961)," in Adonis, *La prière et l'épee: essais sur la culture arabe,* trans. Leila Khatib and Anne Wade Minkowski, ed. Anne Wade Minkowski (Paris: Editions Mercure de France, 1993), 171. This is the translation of the 1961 essay quoted in note 7 above, undertaken in close collaboration with Adonis (see p. 372). It should be noted, however, that the passage I quote here from "Introduction to the History of the Petty Kings" has been changed by Adonis in the 1996 edition to: "We carry the past like a dying shaykh/We regard the future perplexed and with longing." On

God in Adonis, see, Asʿad Khairallah, "Ishmael Must Be Sacrificed: Adūnīs and the Quest for a New God," in *Myths, Historical Archetypes and Symbolic Figures in Arabic Literature: Towards a New Hermeneutic Approach,* ed. Angelika Neuwirth (Beirut: Orient-Institut der DMG; Stuttgart: Franz Steiner for the DMG, 1999), 147–59; and Stefan Weidner, "The Divinity of the Profane. Representations of the Divine in the Poetry of Adûnîs" in *Representations of the Divine in Arabic Poetry,* ed. Gert Borg and Ed de Moor (Amsterdam: Rodopi, 2001), 211–25. On Adonis's sources in the Islamic tradition, see also Kāẓim Jihād, *Adūnīs muntaḥilan: dirāsa fī al-istiḥwādh al-adabī wa irtijāliyyat al-tarjama,* yusbiquhā *Mā huwa al-tanaṣṣ* (Casablanca: Afrīqiyā al-Sharq, 1991; revised and enlarged, Cairo: Maktabat Madbūlī, 1993).

13. Adonis, "Le poète arabe contemporain face à l'héritage," 172.

14. Adonis, "Introduction" to *Fātiḥa li-nihāyāt al-qarn (ṭabaʿa munaqqaḥa wa mazīda)* (Beirut: Dār al-Nahār, 1988), 13.

15. See Atef Faddul, *The Poetics of T. S. Eliot and Adunis* (Beirut: al-Hamra, 1993).

16. Margaret Dickie, *On the Modernist Long Poem* (Iowa City: Univ. of Iowa Press, 1986), 8.

17. Walt Whitman, "A Backward Glance o'er Travel'd Roads," in *Leaves of Grass* [1892 ed.] (New York: Bantam, 1983), 447.

18. Justin Kaplan, "Introduction," in Whitman, *Leaves of Grass,* xvii.

19. Adapting and paraphrasing Kaplan, "Introduction," in *Leaves of Grass,* xvi.

20. Gamāl ʿAbd al-Nāṣir, *Falsafat al-thawra* (Cairo: al-Dār al-Qawmiyya li al-Ṭibāʿa wa al-Nashr, n.d.), 51.

21. In the aftermath of the horrendous events of 11 September 2001, a number of American intellectuals quoted these lines in their newspaper and journal articles. See, for example, Michael Scott Doran, "Somebody Else's Civil War," *Foreign Affairs* 81, no. 1 (2002): 22; and Adam Shatz, "An Arab Poet Who Dares to Differ," *New York Times,* July 13, 2002. I am grateful to Barak Mendelsohn for the Doran reference.

22. Adonis, "Thoughts on the Problems of Poetic Expression and Communication in the Arab Society," *Lotus* 23 (1975): 77.

23. See *The Selected Prose of T. S. Eliot,* ed. Frank Kermode (New York: Harcourt, Brace and Jovanovich, 1975), 43.

24. See, for example, Aḥmad Bassām al-Sāʿī, *Ḥarakat al-shiʿr al-ḥadīth min khilāl aʿlāmihi fī Sūriyā* (Damascus: Dār al-Maʾmūn li al-Turāth, 1978), 123; Aḥmad Dāwūd, *Lughat al-shiʿr* (Damascus: Ittiḥād al-Kuttāb, 1980), 273; Munīr al-ʿIksh, "al-

Shiʿr bayna ḥarakat al-khalq wa al-istijāba," *Mawāqif* 13–14 (1971): 27 [17–39] For ripostes, see, for example, Nayef El-Hasan, "The Complex Poem in New Arabic Poetry 1950–1985" (Ph.D. diss., Univ. of Pennsylvania, 1985), 82–88; and Usayma Darwīsh, *Masār al-taḥawwulāt: qirāʾa fi shiʿr Adūnīs* (Beirut: Dār al-Ādāb, 1992). Darwīsh's work focusses largely on "This Is My Name," as does Khālida Saʿid, "Īqāʿ al-shawq wa al-tajādhub," *Mawāqif* 7 (1970): 250–71, reprinted in her *Ḥarakiyyat al-ibdāʿ* (Beirut: Dār al-ʿAwda, 1979), 87–119.

25. Adonis, "Fātiḥa li-nihāyāt al-qarn," 337.

26. See further my "Walt Whitman in Adonis' Manhattan: Some thoughts on *A Grave for New York,*" *Periodica Islamica* 6, no. 2 (1996): 15–20; cf. Roger Asselineau and Ed Folsom, "Whitman and Lebanon's Adonis," *Walt Whitman Quarterly Review* 15 (1998): 180–84.

27. In all cases, the rereading of and intersection with Whitman is through the prism of Roger Asselineau's French translations, "Le Chant de Soi-Même" and "Les Dormeurs." See Walt Whitman, *Feuilles d'Herbe (choix),* trans. Roger Asselineau (Paris: Société «Les Belles Lettres», 1956).

28. Walt Whitman, *Leaves of Grass* [1892 ed.] (New York and Toronto: Bantam, 1983), 42. I have signalled other significant uses of Whitman in the "Notes to the Translation." Note that just as "Song of Myself" and "The Sleepers" are divided into parts (fifty-two and eight, respectively), so too is "A Grave for New York" divided into parts (ten).

29. This and the following quotation are from Salma Jayyusi, "Contemporary Arab Poetry: Visions and Attitudes," in *Studies in Modern Arabic Literature,* ed. Robin C. Ostle (Warminster: Aris and Phillips, 1975), 53.

30. Adonis, *Muqaddima li al-shiʿr al-ʿArabī* (Beirut: Dār al-ʿĀwda, 1971), 117.

31. Roland Barthes, *The Pleasure of the Text,* trans. R. Miller (London: Jonathan Cape), 14. Cf. Abu Deeb, "The Perplexity of the All-knowing: A Study of Adonis," in *Critical Perspectives in Modern Arabic Literature,* ed. Issa J. Boullata (Washington, D.C.: Three Continents Press, 1980), 309.

32. Adonis, "Fātiḥa li-nihāyāt al-qarn," 339.

33. Khālida Saʿīd, "Īqāʿ al-shawq wa al-tajādhub," 254 (passage translated in Roger Allen, *Modern Arabic Literature* [New York: Ungar, 1987], 37).

34. Basim Musallam, *The Arabs: A Living History* (London: Collins/Harvill, 1983), 34.

APPENDIX A. *Differences Between the 1972 and 1996 Rescensions*

꼬,

Pagination refers to the 1972 edition as included in the facing page Arabic in this volume. References in parentheses are to the 1996 edition.

Muqaddima li-tārīkh mulūk al-ṭawāʿif
Pages 14, line 6–15, line 6

في حصار المذابح . . . ماذا ، قُتِلتْ ؟

أنظرِ الآنَ كيف انتهيتَ ولم تنتهِ المهزله
مُتُّ كالآخرينْ
مثلما ينسجُ الدهرُ في رئة السالفينْ
مثلما يكسر الغيم أبوابه القُزَحِيّه
مثلما يغرق الماءُ في الرمل ِ أو تقطعُ الأبديه
عُنُقَ القُبَّره

have been substituted with two lines (247.3–4):

بين عنق الذبيح و مقصلة الذابحين ؟
كيف ماذا ، قُتِلتْ ؟

Between the neck of the slaughtered and the guillotine of the slaughterers?
How, what? Were you butchered too?

Page 22, line 3:

The word أفراحه has been substituted with لأبعاده (250.2). Thus, "We listened to their celebrations" has been changed to "We listened to their measures."

Page 22, Line 4:

The word راقدون has been substituted with آمنون (250.3). Thus, "sleep as dreams sleep" has been changed to "peaceful as dreams sleep."

Page 22, Line 7:

من أينَ ، هل البحر قادرٌ ، هل حَنانُ الشمس ؟

has been omitted entirely: it would have been at 250.6.

Page 23
Of lines 2–7:

/ هل الشجَرُ الذابلُ يزهو ؟ /

(- متى أتوا ؟ كيف لم نشعرْ ؟ جبال الخليل
يدفعها الليل ويمضي والأرضُ تهزأ / لم نشعر/ دمٌ نازفٌ / هنا
سقط الثائرُ / حيفا تئنُ في حجَرٍ اسودَ و النخلة التي فيَّأت
مريمَ تبكي / حيفا تسافر في عَينيْ قتيلٍ حيفا بحيرة حزن
جرحت قلبها وسالتْ مع الشمس إلينا

only the following remain (250.12–13)

هنا سقط الثائرُ حيفا تئنُ في حجَرٍ اسودَ
و النخلة التي فيَّأت مريمَ تبكي

The revolutionary fell here. Haifa groans in a black rock
and the date palm that gave shade to Mary cries

Page 24

Of lines 1–5:

في الزمنِ القاتل شخصٌ رمى تاريخه للنار غطّى مدى وجوهنا
بحمرة الخجل ْ

وماتَ /
لن تعرفَ حريةٌ ما دامت الدولةُ موجودةٌ /

تذكرُ ؟ كان السجن بوابةٌ للشمس كان الأمل ْ

Only the following remain, with two changes (250.18–19):

في الزمنِ الرماد شخصٌ رمى تاريخه لجمر ايامنا وماتَ
(لن تعرفَ حريةٌ ما دامت الدولةُ موجودة)

In the time of ashes a person threw his history to the embers of our days and died
(You shall not know freedom as long as the State exists)

Page 27

The 1996 edition (252.3) adds the following line between lines 5 and 6:

ماذا يقول الآخرون

This is essentially a repetition of the preceding line: "What do the others say?"

Page 30

Lines 1–4 are omitted in the 1996 edition, as follows:

حيث وقفَ على طرف العمل ، وضع الكتاب كالشامة
على جبينه ورسم جوقةً من الملائكة على شفتيه وأذنيه ، أخذ
يغرز أصابع و اسنانه في قصعة الكلام طالت أذناه و سقط
شعره و تحول

Page 34

The seven lines on this page:

. . ها غزالُ التاريخ يفتحُ أحشائيَ / نهرُ العبيد يهدرُ لم يبقَ
نبيٌّ إلا تصعُلكَ لم يبقَ إلهٌ / نجيءٌ نكتشف الخبز / اكتشفنا
ضوءاً يقود ألى الأرض اكتشفنا شمساً تجيءٌ من القبضة هاتو فؤوسكم
نحمل الله كشيخٍ يموت نفتح للشمس طريقاً غيرَ المآذن للطفل
كتاباً غيرَ الملائك للحلم عيناً غير المدينة والكوفة / هاتوا
فؤوسكم

لستُ وحدي . . .

are condensed and changed to:

. . . ها غزالُ التاريخ يفتحُ أحشائيَ نهرُ العبيد
يهدرُ يحتاج اكتشفنا ضوءاً يقود ألى الأرض اكتشفنا شمساً
تجيءٌ من القبضة هاتو فؤوسكم نحمل الماضي كشيخٍ
يموت نستشرف الآتي هياماً ورغبة

لستُ وحدي . . .

. . . Here is the gazelle of history, opening my entrails The river of slaves
rumbles, needs. We discovered a light leading us to Earth, we discovered a sun
coming from the fist Bring your axes We carry the past like a dying shaykh
We regard the future perplexed and with longing

I am not alone . . .

Note the significant change from "we carry God like a dying shaykh"

نحمل الله كشيخٍ يموت

to "we carry the past like a dying shaykh"
نحمل الماضي كشيخٍ يموت .

Hādha huwa ismī

Page 40, line 9:

The word أفعى has been substituted with ليلا (224.1). Thus, "I have what makes vipers of the green branches" has been changed to "I have what makes a night of the green branches."

Page 57
Of lines 8–11:

أنتَ مملوكٌ هيَ المالكُ ^/] انفصلْ

عن مسارات خطاها تَضِع تَغَرُّب تصرْ غولاً تصرْ

مَسلخاً هي الحلمُ والحالمُ وهْيَ] الملاكُ / [ترتسمُ الأمة] فيها

كبزرةٍ /

Only the following remain, with changes (233.4–5):

أنتَ مملوك

ُ هيَ المالكُ الملاك غد الامة فيها كبذرة

> *You are the subject,*
> *it the proprietary sovereign. The nation's tomorrow is in it like a seed.*

Qabr min ajl New York

Page 71, line 5:
The word أربعة (four) has been corrected to أربع (107.5).

Page 73, line 10:
The plural النباتات (plants) has been changed to the collective النبات (109.1).

Page 78, lines 7–10:
These have been omitted entirely:

و أغري ببروت وأخواتها العواصم ،

تقفز من سريرها و تغلق جلفها أبواب الذكرى . تدنو ،

تتعلّق بقصائدي، وتتدلّى. الفأس للرتاج والزهر للنافذة،

واحترقْ يا تاريخ الأقفال .

They would have commenced at 113.12.

Page 81, line 1:
The word العصر (age) has been changed (corrected?) to العمر (also: age) (115.5).

Page 81, line 7:
The word الميتة (dead) has been changed to تموت (dying) (115.10).

Page 83, line 9:
The word حقدك (your hatred) has been changed to غضبك (your anger) (116.18).

Page 85, line 10:
The word وديانا (riverbeds) has been emended to أوديةٌ (also: riverbeds) (118.11).

Page 86, line
The words كغراب (like a crow) have been emended to غراباً (as/like a crow) (118.15).

Page 87, line 10:
Because the particles are interchangeable, I have not indicated the following change in the Arabic text: ما يزال (to still be) has been changed twice to لا يزال (119.17–18).

Page 87, line 15:
The verb أستبدل (replace) has been changed to أبدلُ (substitute) (120.2).

Page 90, line 16:
The verb سنستبدل (replace) has been changed to سنبدلُ (substitute) (123.19).

Page 94, line 8:
The phrase لنرفع الفأس has been omitted. It would have occurred in 127.6.

Throughout all poems:
In the 1988 and 1996 revisions of the poems, Adonis dispenses with the slashes that punctuate (literally) the 1972 rescension and printing. In the new rescensions, he also omits the dedication to Nasser that appears beneath the title in earlier rescensions.

APPENDIX B. *Publication History of Poems*

✦

1970 *Waqt bayna al-ramād wa al-ward.* 2d ed. Beirut: Manshūrāt Mawāqif,
      1971. Also: Dār al-ʿAwda, 1970.

"Muqaddima li-tārīkh mulūk al-ṭawāʾif"	pp. 7–37
"Hādhā huwa ismī"	pp. 39–69

"Muqaddima" was also included in the following collection:

1971 *Kitābāt ʿalā qabr ʿAbd al-Nāṣir.*
      Ed. ʿAbd al-Muʿṭī al-Ḥijāzī. Beirut: Dār al-ʿAwda.

"Muqaddima li-tārīkh mulūk al-ṭawāʾif"	pp. 43–66

*1972 *Waqt bayna al-ramād wa al-ward.* Beirut: Dār al-ʿAwda.

"Muqaddima li-tārīkh mulūk al-ṭawāʾif"	pp. 5–35
"Hādhā huwa ismī"	pp. 37–67
"Qabr min ajli New York"	pp. 69–97

Included in: *al-Āthār al-kāmila: shiʿr.* 2 vols. Beirut: Dār al-ʿAwda, 1971.
Reprinted as: *al-Aʿmāl al-shiʿriyya al-kāmila.* 2 vols. 2d ed. Beirut: Dār
al-ʿAwda, 1975. 3d ed., 1979. 4th ed., 1985. 5th ed., 1988:

"Muqaddima li-tārīkh mulūk al-ṭwāʾif"	vol. 2, pp. 251–67
"Hādhā huwa ismī"	vol. 2, pp. 268–87
"Qabr min ajli New York"	vol. 2, pp. 288–312

*Edition used for this translation and produced on facing pages.

1980   *Hādhā huwa ismī.* Beirut: Dār al-Ādāb. 2nd ed, 1988.

"Muqaddima li-tārīkh mulūk al-ṭawāʾif"   pp. 7–23
"Hādhā huwa ismī"   pp. 25–45
"Qabr min ajli New York"   pp. 47–74

1996   *al-Aʿmāl al-shiʿriyya,* 3 vols. Damascus: Dār al-Madā li al-Thaqāfa wa al-Nashr, 1996:

Vol. 2: *Hādhā huwa ismī wa qaṣāʾid ukhrā:*

"Hādhā huwa ismī"   pp. 221–39
"Muqaddima li-tārīkh mulūk al-ṭawāʾif"   pp. 241–56

Vol. 3: *Mufrad bi-ṣīghat al-jamʿ wa qaṣāʾid ukhrā:*

"Qabr min ajli New York"   pp. 105–29

GLOSSARY

Abul ʿAla: See *Maʿarri.*

al-Andalus: The medieval Arabic name for Spain. See also *Ibn Jahwar.*

Ali: ʿAli ibn Abi Talib was cousin and son-in-law of the prophet Muhammad and the fourth caliph (656–661) of Islam. The view that ʿAli should have been the first caliph as rightful heir and successor to Muhammad is the starting point of the rift between the Shiʿites, who hold this view, and the Sunnis, who do not. ʿAli is traditionally identified as the father of divination; he is said to have transmitted this esoteric knowledge to his descendants in the form of a book.

Ali ibn Muhammad: Known also as Sahib al-Zanj ("Leader of the Zanj"), ʿAli led an African slave rebellion in southern Iraq between 868 and 883. He is said to have been of Arab origin and to have rejected Sunni orthodoxy. He refused a free pardon after the rebellion was quelled and died in battle.

Ashrafiyya: al-Ashrafiyya, Raʾs Beirut, and Zahrat al-Ihsan are all areas of Beirut.

bâ-jîm-hâ-alif-râ: Five letters of the Arabic alphabet that do not spell a known word in that sequence. They may have divinatory significance. See also *sâd-ʿayn-yâ-hâ-kâf.*

Bonnefoy, Yves: (b. 1923) Regarded as the most important poet to have emerged in France in the Second World War. He is also a literary and art critic, and translator of English poetry and drama, notably Shakespeare. He and Adonis have a friendship of long-standing.

Buthayna: The woman with whom the poet Jamil was in love. See also *Jamil.*

Caliph: The title *(Khalifa)* given to the leader of the Muslim *umma,* or community. No one has held this title since the fall of the Ottoman Empire in the early twentieth century.

dâl, qâf: Two Arabic letters that, in combination, spell numerous words, including the verbs "to pulverize" and "to resound." The word for "minute" (of time), *daqiqa,* can also be formed from these letters.

dissenters: Adonis uses the term *rafidun.* It is a term used by Sunnis to describe people who reject Sunni orthodoxy, typically the Shi'ites. The word also simply means "the refusers." See also *Ali.*

Hallaj: Mansur al-Hallaj was a famous mystic and theologian executed for heretical beliefs in 922. Among his many controversial statements was *"ana al-haqq,"* meaning "I am the eternal verity"—that is, God.

Hamza: The name for the Arabic letter that represents the glottal stop, occurring in numerous words, such as Qur'an. It is also the name of an uncle of the Prophet Muhammad who became a stalwart supporter of his nephew and the nascent Muslim community.

Hayek and Kamal Press: The publisher of Adonis's journal *Mawaqif.*

Ibn 'Abbad: An Arab judge who was proclaimed ruler of Seville in 1024. His reign was marked by disputes with Ibn Jahwar. See also *Ibn Jahwar.*

Ibn Jahwar: A vizier installed in 1031 by the people of Córdoba as governor after the ousting of the royal family. He headed a democratic and peaceful government. Like Ibn 'Abbad, he lived during the period of the disintegration of the Spanish Umayyad caliphate and the political dismemberment of Spain at the hands of the so-called "Petty Kings."

Imrul Qays: A prince and bon vivant who became the most celebrated poet of the pre-Islamic period and who is widely regarded as the greatest Arab poet tout court. He died some time around 540.

Jamil: A seventh-century Arab poet who is regarded as the best representative of ʿUdhri poetry, celebrating chaste and idealized love.

Junayd: An early and very influential Sufi mystic poet of Baghdad. He died in 910.

Kâf-tâ-alif-bâ: Arabic letters of the alphabet that spell the Arabic word *kitāb,* "book."

Kazimiyya: The township of al-Kazimayn near Baghdad. A number of Shiʿite spiritual leaders (*imams*), notably the eponymous Musa al-Kazim (d. 802), are buried there. This Musa, who is also mentioned in "Introduction to the History of the Petty Kings," was a direct descendant of ʿAli ibn Abi Talib.

Kufa: The people of Kufa, Iraq, numbered among ʿAli ibn Abi Talib's staunchest supporters.

Lâm-mîm-alif: Arabic letters that spell the word *lima,* "why?" In reverse sequence, *alif-lâm-mîm,* they are the mystical letters that precede chapter 2, *al-Baqarah* (The cow), of the Qurʾan. There is no scholarly or religious consensus on the import of the various letters that precede Qurʾanic chapters.

Layla: Layla bint Saʿd is a Juliet figure in Arabic literature. She was the beloved of *Qays.*

Maʿarra: See *Maʿarri.*

Maʿarri: Abu al-ʿAla al-Maʿarri (the one from the town of Maʿarra), who died in 1058, was a highly regarded blind poet and prose writer particularly famous for introspective, terse poetry. Adonis has translated some of this poetry into French. See the Bibliography.

Mihrab: The niche or decorative panel in a mosque designating the *qibla,* the direction of Mecca, which Muslims face when performing their ritual prayers.

Mirène: See *Yara.*

Mutanabbi: A poet considered by some to be one of the few challengers to Imrul Qays's hallowed status as the greatest Arab poet. He died in 965.

Nasser, Gamal Abdel: Led the Free Officers' coup that overthrew King Farouk, the British-controlled monarch of Egypt, in 1952. Nasser later became president of Egypt. His pan-Arabism led to the short-lived union of Egypt and Syria as the United Arab Republic (1958–61), and his refusal to align with the West resulted in a major role for Egypt in the Non-Aligned Movement. He built the Aswan High Dam and nationalized the Suez Canal, a factor that contributed to the 1967 War with Israel.

Niffari: A tenth century mystic and philosopher whom Adonis greatly admires. Adonis titled his journal *Mawaqif* (Stations) after al-Niffari's innovative prose work of the same name.

Nimat Allah: A reference to one of two mystics: either Niʿmat Allah ibn Ahmad, who was known as Khalil Sufi (d. 1533), or Niʿmat Allah Wali (d. 1329).

Ninar: See *Yara.*

Petty Kings: A reference to the rulers of the Muslim city-states that arose in Spain in the twelfth century upon the disintegration of the Spanish Umayyad Caliphate. As a result of the strife between the city-states, the period was one of political dismemberment and disunity. The last Muslim city-state, Granada, fell in the Reconquista in 1492.

Qays: The love of Qays ibn Mulawwah for his fellow tribeswoman Layla bint Saʿd is celebrated in the stories of Layla and Majnun Layla. *Majnun,* "mad," here means "the one mad with love for Layla." The pair are often referred to as the Romeo and Juliet figures of Arabic and Islamic literature.

Rabab: A Near Eastern fiddle having one to three strings played with a bow, also known in English as the "rebek."

Ra's Beirut Bookstore: See *Ashrafiyya.*

Sâd-'ayn-yâ-hâ-kâf: In reverse order, the mystical letters that precede chapter 19 of the Qur'an, *Maryam* (Mary). Ibn Abi al-Hadid, a prominent commentator of an anthology of sayings attributed to 'Ali, identifies the sequence as one of the banner-slogans (*shi'ar*) of 'Ali.

Solomon's ant: A reference to the "valley of the ants" mentioned in chapter 27 of the Qur'an, *al-Naml* (The ant).

The Table-Spread: The name of the fifth chapter of the Qur'an, *al-Ma'ida.*

'Urwa ibn al-Ward: An Arab poet who flourished in the pre-Islamic period and who lived into Islamic times. 'Urwa is also remembered for his devotion to the poor.

Yara and Ninar: Yara is the daughter of Mirène Ghossein, a friend (and translator) of Adonis. Ninar is Adonis's younger daughter.

Zahratul Ihsan: See *Ashrafiyya.*

SELECTED BIBLIOGRAPHY

Adonis's Works

POETRY

Dalīla [Delilah]. Damascus: Maṭbaʿat ibn Zaydūn, 1950.

Qālat al-arḍ [The Earth said]. Damascus: Maṭbaʿat Ibn Zaydūn, 1952; revised, 1954.

Qaṣāʾid ūlā [First poems]. Beirut: Dār Majallat Shiʿr, 1957; revised as *Qaṣāʾid ūlā uḍīfa ilayhā qaṣāʾid lam tunshar* [First poems, including previously unpublished poems], 1963; Dār al-ʿAwda, 1970, 1971; revised, Dār al-Ādāb, 1988.

Awrāq fi al-rīḥ [Leaves in the wind]. Beirut: Dār Majallat Shiʿr, 1958, 1963; Dār al-ʿAwda, 1970; revised Dār al-Ādāb, 1988.

Aghānī Mihyār al-Dimashqī [The songs of Mihyar of Damascus]. Beirut: Dār Majallat Shiʿr, 1961; Dār al-ʿAwda, 1970, 1971; revised, Dār al-Ādāb, 1988.

Kitāb al-Taḥawwulāt wa al-hijra fi aqālīm al-nahār wa al-layl [The book of metamorphoses and migration in the regions of day and night]. Beirut: al-Maktabat al-ʿAṣriyya, 1965; Dār al-ʿAwda, 1970; revised, Dār al-Ādāb, 1988.

al-Masraḥ wa al-marāyā [The stage and the mirrors]. Beirut: Dāar al-Ādāb, 1968; revised, Dār al-Ādāb, 1988.

Waqt bayna al-ramād wa al-ward [A time between ashes and roses]. Beirut: Manshūrāt Mawāqif/Dār al-ʿAwda, 1970, enlarged, 1972; revised as *Hādha huwa ismī* [This is my name]. Beirut: Dār al-Ādāb, 1980, 1988.

Dīwān Adūnīs [The collected poetry of Adonis], 2 vols. Beirut: Dār al-ʿAwda, 1971, 1975, 1979; reissued as *al-Aʿmāl al-shiʿriyya al-kāmila* [The complete poetical works], also as *al-Āthār al-kāmila: shiʿr* [The complete works: poetry], 1985, 1988; revised, enlarged, definitive edition, *al-Aʿmāl al-shiʿriyya al-kāmila* [The complete poetical works], 3 vols. Damascus: Dār al-Madā li al-Nashr, 1996: vol. 1: *Aghānī Mihyār al-Dimashqī wa qaṣāʾid ukhrā;* vol. 2: *Hādha huwa ismī wa qaṣāʾid ukhrā;* vol. 3: *Mufrad bi-ṣīghat al-jamʿ wa qaṣāʾid ukhrā.*

Mufrad bi-ṣīghat al-jamʿ [Singular in the form of the plural]. Beirut: Dār al-ʿAwda, 1975; 1977; revised, 1988.

Kitāb al-qaṣāʾid al-khams talīhā *al-Muṭābaqāt wa al-awāʾil* [The book of the five poems, *followed by* Congruences and firsts]. Beirut: Dār al-ʿAwda, 1979; revised, 1988.

Kitāb al-Ḥiṣār: Ḥazīrān 82–Ḥazīrān 85 [The book of the siege, June '82 to June '85]. Beirut: Dār al-Ādāb, 1985.

Shahwa tataqaddam fi kharāʾiṭ al-mādda [Desire advancing in maps of matter]. Casablanca: Dār Tūbqāl li al-Nashr, 1987.

Iḥtifāʾan bi al-ashyāʾ al-wāḍiḥa al-ghāmiḍa [In celebration of things clear-obscure]. Beirut: Dār al-Ādāb, 1988.

Abjadiyya thāniya [A second alphabet]. Casablanca: Dār Tūbqāl li al-Nashr, 1994

al-Kitāb (ams al-makān al-ān. Makhṭūṭah tunsabu ilā al-Mutanabbi) [The book (yesterday of today's now. A manuscript attributed to al-Mutanabbi)], vol. 1. London: Dār al-Sāqī, 1995.

Fihris li-aʿmāl al-rīḥ [A catalog for the wind's deeds]. Beirut: Dār al-Nahār, 1998.

al-Kitāb [The book], vol. 2. London: Dār al-Sāqī, 1998.

al-Mahd (lī fi turāb al-Yaman ʿirqun mā) [The Cradle (I have some root or other in the earth of Yemen]. Sanaʿa: Al-Hayʾa al-ʿĀmma li al-Kitāb, 2001.

AUTOBIOGRAPHICAL

Hā-anta, ayyuhā al-waqt: sīra shiʿriyya thaqāfiyya [Here you are, O Time: a poetic, cultural biography]. Beirut: Dār al-Ādāb, 1993.

CRITICISM (BOOKS)

Muqaddima li al-shiʿr al-ʿarabī [Introduction to Arabic poetry]. Beirut: Dār al-ʿAwda, 1971; multiple editions.

Zaman al-shiʿr [The time of poetry]. Beirut: Dār al-ʿAwda, 1972; multiple editions; revised, 1978; multiple editions.

al-Thābit wa al-mutaḥawwil: baḥth fī al-ibdāʿ wa al-ittibāʿ ʿinda al-ʿArab [The static and the changing: a study of creativity and conformity among the Arabs], 3 vols. Vol. 1: *al-Uṣūl* [The Foundations], Beirut: 1974; vol. 2: *Taʾṣīl al-uṣūl* [Erecting the foundations], Beirut: 1977; vol. 3: *Ṣadmat al-ḥadātha wa sulṭat al-mawrūth al-dīnī* [The shock of modernity and the tyranny of the religious heritage], Beirut: 1978; multiple editions; revised and enlarged in 4 vols., London, Dār al-Sāqī, 1994.

(with others) *Normes et valeurs dans l'Islam contemporain* [Norms and values in contemporary Islam], ed. Paris: Payot, 1996.

Fātiḥa li-nihāyāt al-qarn: bayānāt min ajl thaqāfa ʿarabiyya jadīda [Preface to the century's endings: observations on a new Arabic culture]. Beirut: Dār al-ʿAwda, 1980; revised and enlarged, Dār al-Ādāb, 1998.

al-Shiʿriyya al-ʿarabiyya [Arabic poetics]. Beirut: Dār al-Adāb, 1985.

Siyāsat al-shiʿr: dirāsa fī al-shiʿriyya al-ʿarabiyya al-muʿāṣira [The politics of poetry: a study of contemporary Arabic poetics]. Beirut: Dār al-Ādāb, 1985.

Kalām al-bidāyāt [The speech of beginnings]. Beirut: Dār al-Ādāb, 1989.

al-Ṣūfiyya wa al-sūryāliyya [Sufism and surrealism]. Beirut and London: Dār al-Sāqī, 1992.

al-Naṣṣ al-qurʾānī wa āfāq al-kitāba [The Qurʾanic text and the horizons of writing]. Beirut: Dār al-Ādāb, 1993.

al-Niẓām wa al-kalām [Order and words]. Beirut: Dār al-Ādāb, 1993.

EDITED ANTHOLOGIES

Mukhtārāt min shiʿr Yūsuf al-Khāl [Selections from the poetry of Yūsuf al-Khāl]. Beirut: Dār Majallat Shiʿr, 1962; revised, 1964.

Dīwān al-shiʿr al-ʿarabi [Anthology of Arabic poetry], 3 vols. Beirut: al-Maktabat al-ʿAṣriyya, vol. 1, 1964; vol. 2, 1964; vol. 3, 1968.

Mukhtārāt min shiʿr al-Sayyāb [Selections from the poetry of al-Sayyāb]. Beirut: Dār al-Ādāb, 1967; reissued as *Badr Shākir al-Sayyāb: qaṣāʾid* [Badr Shākir al-Sayyāb: poems], 1978.

(with Khālida Saʿīd), *Mukhtārāt min shiʿr Shawqī* [Selections from the poetry of Shawqī]. Beirut: Dār al-ʿIlm li al-Malāyīn, 1982.

(with Khālida Saʿīd), *Mukhtārāt min shiʿr al-Ruṣāfī* [Selections from the poetry of al-Ruṣāfī]. Beirut: Dār al-ʿIlm li al-Malāyīn, 1982.

(with Khālida Saʿīd), *Mukhtārāt min al-Kawākibī* [Selections from al-Kawākibī]. Beirut: Dār al-ʿIlm li al-Malāyīn, 1982.

(with Khālida Saʿīd), *Mukhtārāt min Muḥammad ʿAbduh* [Selections from Muḥammad ʿAbduh]. Beirut: Dār al-ʿIlm li al-Malāyīn, 1983.

(with Khālida Saʿīd), *Mukhtārāt min Muḥammad Rashīd Riḍā* [Selections from Muḥammad Rashīd Riḍā]. Beirut: Dār al-ʿIlm li al-Malāyīn, 1983.

(with Khālida Saʿīd), *Mukhtārāt min shiʿr Jamīl Ṣidqī al-Zahāwī* [Selections from the poetry of Jamīl Ṣidqī al-Zahāwī]. Beirut: Dār al-ʿIlm li al-Malāyīn, 1983.

(with Khālida Saʿīd), *Mukhtārāt min [nuṣūṣ] al-Imām Muḥammad ibn ʿAbd al-Wahhāb* [Selections from (the texts of) Imām Muḥammad ibn ʿAbd al-Wahhāb]. Beirut: Dār al-ʿIlm li al-Malāyīn, 1983.

TRANSLATIONS

Into Arabic

Georges Schéhadé, *al-Aʿmāl al-masraḥiyya al-kāmila* [*Théâtre complet*]. Kuwait, Wizārat al-Iʿlām: *Ḥikāyat Fāskū* [*Histoire de Vasco*], 1972; *al-Sayyid Būbal* [*Monsieur Boble*], 1972; *al-Muhājir Brīsbān* [*L'émigré de Brisbane*], *1973;* al-Banafsaj [*La Violette*], 1973; *al-Safar* [*Le Voyage*], 1975; *Sahrat al-amthāl* [*La Soirée des proverbes*], 1975; new edition in 6 vols., Beirut, Dār al-Nahār: vol. 1, 2000.

Saint-John Perse, *al-Aʿmāl al-shiʿriyya al-kāmila* [*L'oeuvre poétique complète*]. Damascus: Wizārat al-Thaqāfa al-Qawmī: *Minārāt* [*Amers*], 1976; *Manfā wa qaṣāʾid ukhrā* [*Eloges, La Gloire des rois, Anabase, Exil, Pluies, Poèmes à l'étrangère*], 1978.

Jean Racine, *al-Aʿmāl al-masraḥiyya al-kāmila* [*Théâtre complet*]. Kuwait: Wizārat al-Iʿlām: *Maʾsat Ṭībā aw al-Shaqīqān al-ʿAduwwān* [*La Thébaïde ou les Frères ennemis*], 1972; *Fidra* [*Phèdre*], 1975; revised, 1979.

Yves Bonnefoy, *al-Āʿmāl al-shiʿriyya al-kāmila* [*L'Oeuvre poétique*]. Damascus: Wizārat al-Thaqāfa, 1986.

From Arabic

(with Anne Wade Minkowski), al-Maʿarrī, *Rets d'éternité* [selections from *al-Luzūmiyyāt*]. Paris: Fayard, 1988.

(with Anne Wade Minkowski), Kahlil Gibran, *Le livre des processions* [*al-Mawākib*]. Paris: Arfuyen, 1998.

Translations of Adonis's Poetry into English

Complete or partial translations of the poems from *A Time Between Ashes and Roses* are identified by title.

"Adonis (Ali Ahmed Said): Introduction with some of his translated poetry." Trans. Samuel Hazo and Mirène Ghossein. *Mundus Artium* 3, no. 2 (1970): 6–17.

The Blood of Adonis, Transpositions of Selected Poems of Adonis (Ali Ahmed Said). Trans. Samuel Hazo, Mirène Ghossein, and Kamal Boullata. Pittsburgh: Univ. of Pittsburgh Press, 1971.

Selected poetry. Trans. M. M. Badawi. *Journal of Arabic Literature* 2 (1971): 98–101. Reprinted in *New Writing from the Middle East*. Ed. Leo Hamalian and John D. Yohannan. New York: New American Library [also Ungar], 1978: 65.

"Adonis: A Poet in Lebanon." Trans. Samuel Hazo and Mirène Ghossein. *Books Abroad* 46 (1972): 238–42.

Selected poetry. Trans. Abdullah al-Udhari. In *A Mirror for Autumn*. London:

Menard Press, 1974. Reprinted in *New Writing from the Middle East*. Ed. Leo Hamalian and John D. Yohannan, 64–65. New York: New American Library [also Ungar], 1978.

Selected poetry. Trans. Mounah A. Khoury and Hamid Algar. In *An Anthology of Modern Arabic Poetry*, 195–99. Berkeley: Univ. of California Press, 1974.

Mirrors. Trans. Abdullah al-Udhari. London: TR Press, 1976.

Selected poetry. Trans. Issa J. Boullata. In *Modern Arab Poets*, 67–79. Washington D.C.: Three Continents Press, 1976.

"This Is My Name" [partial]. Trans. Adnan Haydar. *Edebiyat* 1, no. 2 (1977): 141–43.

Selected poetry. Trans. Samuel Hazo. *Mundus Artium* 10, no. 1 (1977): 182–84.

Selected poetry. Trans. Roger Allen. *Nimrod* 24, no. 2 (1980/81): 46–47.

"Translation from the Arabic of poems by Adunis." Trans. John Wain, with the help of Kamal Abu Deeb. MS 2865.5, John Wain Archive, Edinburgh Univ. Library, 1977. 14 typescript pages.

Transformations of the Lover. Pittsburgh: International Poetry Forum, 1982. Including: "The Funeral of New York" [partial]. Trans. Mirène Ghossein, Kamal Boullata, and Samuel Hazo, 59–76. Reprint: Athens: Ohio Univ. Press, 1983. Revised: *The Pages of Day and Night*. Trans. Samuel Hazo, 57–74. Marlboro, Vt.: Marlboro Press, 1994; Reprint: Evanston, Ill.: Marlboro Press/Northwestern Univ. Press, 2000.

Victims of a Map. Mahmud Darwish, Samih al-Qasim, Adonis. Trans. Abdullah al-Udhari, 86–165. London: Al Saqi, 1984.

Selected poetry. Trans. Abdullah al-Udhari. In *Modern Poetry of the Arab World*, 59–75. Harmondsworth, England: Penguin, 1986.

Selected poetry. Trans. Lena Jayyusi and Alan Brownjohn. In *Modern Arabic Poetry: An Anthology*. Ed Salma Khadra Jayyusi, 137–40. New York: Columbia Univ. Press, 1987.

"A Grave for New York" [partial]. Trans. Lena Jayyusi and Alan Brownjohn. In *Modern Arabic Poetry: An Anthology*. Ed Salma Jayyusi, 140–51. New York: Columbia Univ. Press, 1987.

"Language, Culture and Reality." Trans. Nancy Berg, rev. Nur Elmessiri. *Alif* 7 (1987): 113–20.

Selected poetry. *When the Words Burn. An Anthology of Arabic Poetry: 1945–1987.* Trans. John Mikhail Asfour, 159–70. Dunvegan, Ontario: Cormorant Books, 1988.

Love Poems: If Only the Sea Could Sleep. Trans. Kamal Boullata. Interlink, 1989. Reissued as *If Only the Sea Could Sleep.* London: Saqi Books, 2002; Los Angeles: Green Integer, 2003.

"A Grave . . . because of New York" [complete]. Trans. Shawkat M. Toorawa. *Journal of Arabic Literature* 21, no. 1 (1990): 43–56.

Mona Takieddine Amyuni. "Adonis's *Time* Poem: Translation and Analysis." *Journal of Arabic Literature* 21, no. 2 (1990): 172–82.

An Introduction to Arab Poetics. Trans. Catherine Cobham. London: Saqi Books; Austin: Univ. of Texas Press, 1990.

"This Is My Name" [complete]. Trans. Kamal Abu Deeb. *Grand Street* 40 (1991): 151–65. (Also archived at <http://www.jehat.com/english/adonis-bio-3e.htm>)

"Introduction to the History of the Petty Kings" [complete]. Trans. Shawkat M. Toorawa. *Journal of Arabic Literature* 23, no. 1 (1992): 27–35.

Beginnings. Trans. Kamal Boullata and Mirène Ghossein. Washington, D.C.: Pyramid Atlantic, 1992 [Limited edition].

"This Is My Name" [complete]. Trans. Shawkat M. Toorawa. *Journal of Arabic Literature* 24, no. 1 (1993): 28–38.

Selected poetry. Trans. K. Mattawa. *International Quarterly* 1, no. 3 (1994): 126–27.

"A Grave for New York" [complete]. Trans. Kamal Abu Deeb. Archived at: <http://www.jehat.com/english/adonis-bio-3b.htm> [1996?]

Selected poetry. *aljadid* 2, no. 3 (1996): 16–17.

Selected poetry. *aljadid* 2, no. 9 (1996): 17.

Selected poetry. Trans. A. al-Udhari. *Index on Censorship* 26 (1997): 32–34.

Selected poetry. *Jusur* 9–10 (1997–98): 426–36 [trans. H. Haddawy]; 137–51 [trans. Adnan Haydar and Michael Beard].

Selected poetry. *aljadid* 4, no. 23 (1998): 28.

Selected poetry. Trans. Kamal Abu Deeb. *Banipal,* no. 1 (1998): 3–7.

Selected poetry. *Banipal,* no. 2 (1998): 34, 35, 36, 37, 38, 39 [trans. Sargon Boulos], 40 [trans. Adnan Haydar].

Selected poetry. Trans. H. Hilmy. Archived at: <http://www.geocities.com/hhilmy_ma/toc.html> [1998?]

Selected poetry. Trans. Marilyn Hacker with Vénus Khoury-Ghata. *Banipal,* no. 10–11 (2001): 126–28.

Selected poetry. Trans. Ferial Ghazoul. *aljadid* 8, no. 39 (2002): 16

Studies, Criticism, and Analyses of (and by) Adonis in English

Abu Deeb, Kamal. In *Encyclopedia of Arabic Literature.* Ed. Julie Scott Meisami and Paul Starkey. 2 vols. London and New York: Routledge, 1998: vol. 1: 57–59.

———. "From Static Harmony to Dynamic Contradiction. The Contradictory Visions of the Unified but Not Unitarian Self: A Contradictory Study of Adonis" [1998?] Archived at: http://www.jehat.com/english/studies-1.htm

———. "The Perplexity of the All-knowing: A Study of Adonis." *Mundius Artium* 10, no. 1 (1977): 163–81. Reprinted in *Critical Perspectives in Modern Arabic Literature.* Ed. Issa J. Boullata, 305–23. Washington, D.C.: Three Continents Press, 1980.

Adonis. *Introduction to Arab Poetics.* Trans. Catherine Cobham. Austin: Univ. of Texas Press, 1990.

———. "Thoughts on the Problems of Poetic Expression and Communication in the Arab Society." *Lotus* 23 (1975): 62–84.

Ajami, Fouad. *The Dream Palace of the Arabs: A Generation's Odyssey.* New York: Pantheon Books, 1998: 112–14, 143–46, 164–65, 253–55.

Allen, Roger. *The Arabic Literary Heritage: The Development of Its Genres and Criticism.* Cambridge: Cambridge Univ. Press, 1998: 215–17, 362–63, 405–6.

———. *Modern Arabic Literature.* A Library of Literary Criticism. New York: Ungar, 1987: 29–42.

———. "Adunis." In *The Encyclopedia of World Literature in the 20th Century.* Ed. Leonard S. Klein, 15–17. Rev. ed. New York: Ungar, 1981: Volume 1.

AshShareef, Teirab. "The Metamorphic Vision: The Poetics of Time and History in the Works of Adunis (ʿAli Ahmad Saʿid)." Ph.D. dissertation, Indiana Univ., 1986.

Asfour, John M. "Introduction" in *When the Words Burn. An Anthology of Modern Arabic Poetry: 1945–1987*. Dunvegan, Ontario: Cormorant Books: esp. 36–60.

———. "Adonis and Muhammad al-Maghut: Two Voices in a Burning Land." *Journal of Arabic Literature* 20, no. 1 (1989): 20–30.

Asselineau, Roger, and Ed Folsom. "Whitman and Lebanon's Adonis." *Walt Whitman Quarterly Review* 15 (1998): 180–84.

Badawi, M. M. *A Critical Introduction to Modern Arabic Poetry*. Cambridge: Cambridge Univ. Press, 1975: 231–41.

———. *A Short History of Modern Arabic Literature*. Oxford: Clarendon Press, 1993: 74–81.

Boullata, Issa J. "Adonis: Revolt in Modern Arabic Poetics." *Edebiyat* 2, no. 1 (1977): 1–13.

———. "Textual Intentions: A Reading of Adonis' Poem 'Unintended Worship Ritual.' " *International Journal of Middle East Studies* 21, no. 4 (1989): 541–62.

Corrao, F. M. "Adonis' Perspective on the Reading of Arabic Poetry." In *Studies in Arabic and Islam. Proceedings of the 19th Congress, Union Européenne des Arabisants et Islamisants,* Halle, 1998. Ed. S. Leder with H. Kilpatrick, B. Martel-Thoumain and H. Schönig, 175–84. Leuven: Peeters, 2002.

DeYoung, Terri. "Upon One Double String: The Metaphysical Element in Adūnīs's Poetry." *Al-ʿArabiyya* 27 (1994): 1–15.

———. "Introduction to the History of the Petty Kings by Adunis." In *Middle Eastern Literatures and Their Times*. Ed. Joyce Moss, 209–20. Detroit: Thomson Gale, 2004.

El-Hasan, Nayef Khaled. "The Complex Poem in New Arabic Poetry, 1950–1985." Ph.D. dissertation, Univ. of Pennsylvania, 1985: esp. 82–88.

Faddul, Atef. *The Poetics of T. S. Eliot and Adunis*. Beirut: Al-Hamra Publishers, 1993.

Haydar, Adnan. "Making Mihyar: The Familiarization of Adunis's Knight of Strange Words." *Literature East & West* 4, nos. 1–2 (1988): *Critical Pilgrimages: Studies in the Arabic Literary Tradition,* 79–88.

Ibrahim, Dawood. "The Unconscious in the Poetic Theories and Practice of Robert Bly and Adonis (Ali Ahmad Said)." *Abhath al-Yarmouk: Humanities & Social Sciences* 12, no. 1 (1994): 67–83.

Jayyusi, Salma K. *Trends and Movements in Modern Arabic Poetry.* 2 vols. Leiden: E. J. Brill, 1977: vol. 2, esp. 625ff. and 649ff.

Khairallah, Asʿad. "Ishmael Must Be Sacrificed: Adūnīs and the Quest for a New God." In *Myths, Historical Archetypes, and Symbolic Figures in Arabic Literature: Towards a New Hermeneutic Approach.* Ed. Angelika Neuwirth. Beirut: Orient-Institut der DMG; Stuttgart: Franz Steiner, 1999: 147–59.

Khazali, Mohammad Mohmoud. "Modernity: A Study of Adūnīs' Theory and Poetry." Ph.D. dissertation, Univ. of Texas at Austin, 1983.

Khouri, Mounah A. "A Critique of Adonis's Perspectives on Arabic Literature and Culture." In Mounah A. Khouri, *Studies in Contemporary Arabic Poetry and Criticism.* Middle East Book Series 16. Piedmont, Calif.: Jehan Book Co., 1987: 13–41. Published in abbreviated form as "Criticism and the Heritage: Adonis as an Advocate of a New Arab Culture." In *Arab Civilization: Challenges and Responses. Studies in Honor of Constantine K. Zurayk.* Ed. George N. Atiyeh and Ibrahim M. Oweiss. Albany: State Univ. of New York Press, 1988: 183–207.

Lee, Dennis. *Reading Adonis.* Toronto: Coach House Press, 1987.

Obank, Margaret, and Samuel Shimon. "Adonis: There Are Many Easts in the East and Many Wests in the West" [Interview with Adonis]. *Banipal,* no. 2 (1998), 30–40.

Said, Aly Ahmad [Adonis]. "The Contemporary Arab Poet and the Three Attitudes Towards Freedom." *Afro-Asian Writings* 1, nos. 2–3 (1968): 119–22.

Saʿīd, Khālida. "The Power of the Word." 50 mins. Director: Colin Luke. A VATV Production in association with Kufic Films B.V., 1982. [Companion vol.: Basim Musallam, *The Arabs: A Living History.* London: Collins/Harvill, 1983.]

al-Sharᶜ, ᶜAli Ahmad. "An Analytical Study of the Adonisian Poem." Ph.D.
dissertation, Univ. of Michigan, 1982: esp. 237–56.

Snir, Reuven. "A Study of Elegy for al-Ḥallāj by Adūnīs." *Journal of Arabic Lit-
erature* 25, no. 3 (1994): 245–56.

Starkey, Paul J. "Adunis." In *Encyclopedia of Literary Translation into English.*
2000. Ed. Olive Classe, 3–4. London, Chicago: Fitzroy Dearborn, 2000.

al-Tami, Ahmed Salih. "The Poetic Theories of the Leading Poet-Critics of
Arabic New Poetry." Ph.D. dissertation, Univ. of Michigan, 1989.

Toorawa, Shawkat M. "Adunis." In *Reference Guide to World Literature. Vol. 1:
Authors,* 3d ed. Ed. Sara and Tom Pendergast, 6–9. Detroit: St. James
Press, 2002.

———. 'Walt Whitman in Adonis' Manhattan: Some Thoughts on *A Grave
for New York." Periodica Islamica* 6 (1996): 15–20.

———. "A Critical Translation of *Waqt bayna al-ramād wa al-ward.*" M.A. the-
sis, Univ. of Pennsylvania, 1989.

Weidner, Stefan. "The Divinity of the Profane: Representations of the Di-
vine in the Poetry of Adûnîs." In *Representations of the Divine in Arabic Po-
etry.* Ed. Gert Borg and Ed de Moor, 211–25. Amsterdam, Atlanta:
Rodopi, 2001.

———. "A Guardian of Change? The Poetry of Adûnîs Between Hermeti-
cism and Commitment." In *Conscious Voices: Concepts of Writing in the
Middle East.* Ed. Stephan Guth et al. Stuttgart: Franz Steiner, 1999:
277–92.

Zeidan, Joseph. "Myth and Symbol in the Poetry of Adūnīs and Yūsuf al-
Khāl." *Journal of Arabic Literature* 10 (1979): 70–94.

Selected Additional Reading

Adonis has received considerable critical attention in Europe, especially
France. More translations of his work have appeared in French than in any
other language, and numerous journals have devoted parts of or whole issues
to Adonis. What follows is a partial listing; a comprehensive bibliography may
be found in *Adonis: Un poète dans le monde d'aujourd'hui, 1950–2000,* 322–27.

ʿAbd al-Nāṣir, Gamāl. *Falsafat al-thawra*. Cairo: al-Dār al-Qawmiyya li al-Ṭibāʿa wa al-Nashr, n.d.

Abū Fakhr, Ṣaqr. *Ḥiwā maʿa Adūnīs: al-ṭufūla, al-shiʿr, al-manfā*. Beirut: al-Muʿassasa al-ʿArabiyya li al-Dirāsāt wa al-Nashr, 2000.

Adonis. *Epitafio para Nueva York—Marrakech/Fez*. Trans. Federico Arbós. Madrid: Hiperión, 1987.

————. *Newyorkʿa mezar*. Trans. Özdemir Ince. Istanbul: Varlık Vayınları, 1989.

————. *Le Prophète*, preface by Adonis. Trans. Anne Wade Minkowski. Paris: Gallimard, 1992.

————. *La prière et l'épee: essais sur la culture arabe*. Trans. Leila Khatib and Anne Wade Minkowski. Paris: Editions Mercure de France, 1993.

————. *Tombeau pour New York*, suivi de *Prologue à l'histoire des rois des tâ'ifa* et de *Ceci est mon nom*. Trans. Anne Wade Minkowski. Paris: Editions Sindbad, 1986. Reprint: Actes Sud/Sindbad, 1999.

————. *Toucher la lumière*. Trans. Anne Wade Minkowski. Paris: Imprimerie nationale, 2003.

Adonis. Un poète dans le monde d'aujourd'hui, 1950–2000. Paris: Institut du monde arabe, 2000. [The companion catalog to a retrospective exhibition of Adonis's poetry, criticism, translation, and art and held at the Institut du monde arabe in Paris from 11 Dec. 2000 to 18 Feb. 2001.]

Al-Maqaleh, Abdel-Aziz. "Tombeau pour New York. Tombeau pour la domination et le racisme." In *Adonis: Un poète dans le monde d'aujourd'hui, 1950–2000*, 60–65. Paris: Institut du monde arabe, 2000.

Balqāsim, Khālid, *Adūnīs wa al-khiṭāb al-Ṣūfī*. Casablanca: Dār Tūbqāl li al-Nashr, 2000.

Bishop, Michael. "Profondes marginalités: D'Adonis, Stéfan et Bancquart à Chedid, Rognet et Stétié." *L'esprit créateur* 38, no. 1 (1998): 91–102.

Būmashūlī, ʿAbd al-ʿAzīz, *al-Shiʿr wa al-taʾwīl: qirāʿa fī shiʿr Adūnīs*. Casablanca: Afrīqiyā al-Sharq, 1998.

Camus, Michel. *Adonis, le visionnaire: essai et anthologie*. Monaco: Editions du Rocher, 2000.

Darwīsh, Usayma. *Taḥrīr al-maʿnā: dirāsa naqdiyya fi dīwān Adūnīs: al-Kitāb I.* Beirut: Dār al-Ādāb, 1997.

———. *Masār al-taḥawwulāt: qirāʾ a fī shiʿr Adūnīs.* Beirut: Dār al-Ādāb, 1992.

Détours d'écriture, no. 16 (1991): *Adonis, le feu souterrain.* [Special issue devoted entirely to Adonis.]

Doran, Michael Scott. "Somebody Else's Civil War." *Foreign Affairs* 81, no. 1 (2002): 22.

Elfadel, Ibrahim M. "L'Equation comme 'Tombeau pour New York.'" In *Adonis: Un poète dans le monde d'aujourd'hui, 1950–2000,* 300. Paris: Institut du monde arabe, 2000.

Elmarsafy, Ziad. "Ceci est mon nom, ceci est mon idiome." In *Adonis: Un poète dans le monde d'aujourd'hui, 1950–2000,* 123. Paris: Institut du monde arabe, 2000.

Ghālī, Wāʾil. *al-Shiʿr wa al-fikr: Adūnīs namūdhajan.* Cairo: al-Hayʾa al-Miṣriyya al-ʿĀmma li al-Kitāb, 2001.

al-ʿIksh, Mūnir. "al-Shiʿr bayna ḥarakat al-khalq wa al-istijāba." *Mawāqif* 13–14 (1971): 17–39.

Irwin, Robert, trans. *Night and Horses and the Desert: An Anthology of Classical Arabic Literature.* London: Allen Lane, 1999; New York: Anchor Books, 2000.

Ismāʿīl, ʿAbd al-Fattāḥ. *al-Turāth wa al-thaqāfa al-waṭaniyya: naṣṣ ḥiwār al-shāʿir Adūnīs maʿa ʿAbd al-Fattāḥ Ismāʿīl.* Beirut: Dār Ibn Khaldūn, 1986.

Jihād, Kāẓim. *Adūnīs muntahilan: dirāsa fi al-istiḥwādh al-adabī wa irtijāliyyat al-tarjama,* yusbiquhā *Mā huwa al-tanāṣṣ.* Casablanca: Afrīqiyā al-Sharq, 1991; revised and enlarged: Cairo: Maktabat Madbūlī, 1993.

Kabbal, Maati. *Le livre des stations de Niffarí,* afterword ("Vers une étrangeté familière") by Adonis. Sommières: Editions de l'éclat, 1989.

Khoury, Nassim. *Introduction à la modernité arabe: essai d'étude critique de l'oeuvre d'Adonis.* Beirut: Dar al-Hadatha, 1986.

Lambarki, Zaari. "Mythes et symboles dans la poésie d'Adonis." Ph.D. dissertation, Univ. of Paris, 1994.

L'œil de bœuf, no. 8 (1995). [Special issue devoted entirely to Adonis.]

Minkowski, Anne Wade. "Biographie d'Adonis." In *Adonis. Un poète dans le monde d'aujourd'hui, 1950–2000,* 202–86. Paris: Institut du monde arabe, 2000.

Qāsim, ʿAdnān Ḥusayn. *al-Ibdāʿ wa maṣādiruhu al-thaqāfiyya ʿinda Adūnīs.* Cairo: al-Dār al-ʿArabiyyali al-Nashr wa al-Tawzīʿ, 2000.

al-Sāʿī, Aḥmad Bassām. *Ḥarakat al-shiʿr al-ḥadīth min khilāl aʿlāmihi fī Sūriyā.* Damascus: Dār al-Maʾmūn li al-Turāth, 1978.

Saʿīd, Khālida. "Īqāʿ al-shawq wa al-tajādhub." *Mawāqif* 7 (1970): 250–71; reprinted in her *Ḥarakiyyat al-ibdāʿ,* 87–119. Beirut: Dār al-ʿAwda, 1979.

———. "Le message du renouveau dans la littérature arabe moderne." Ph.D. dissertation, Univ. of Paris, 1974.

Skarzynska-Bochenska, Krystyna. "La symbolique du bien et du mal dans la poésie d'Adonis." *Rocznik Orientalistyczny* 48, no. 1 (1992): 64–82.

———. "'L'amour et la mort dans la poésie d'Adonis 'L'amour est une aile, La mort est une aile.'" In *Studies in Arabic and Islam: Proceedings of the 19th Congress, Union Européenne des Arabisants et Islamisants, Halle 1998.* Ed. S. Leder with H. Kilpatrick, B. Martel-Thoumian, and H. Schönig, 329–36. Leuven: Peeters, 2002.

Weidner, Stefan. "Adonis." In *Kritisches Lexicon zur fremdsprachigen Gegenwartsliteratur.* Ed. Heinz Ludwig Arnold, 1–11. Munich: Edition Text und Kritik, 1996.

[unknown author]. "La lumière et la couleur dans l'oeuvre d'Adonis (Waqt bayna-l-ramad waʾl-ward)." Ph.D. dissertation, Univ. of Paris III, 1978.